Meals and Memories with Nonno

Rinnovazioni, modificazioni e vidimazion

AMERICAN CONSULATE   No. *5 6 3*

at ____ **NAPLES, ITALY**
   (City)   (Country)

SEEN

For the journey to the United States

via ____

4 GEN 1921

Seal and   (The validity of this visa expires two
ce Stamp   months from this date, provided the pass
     continues to be valid for that period

— I —

Il presente passaporto è valido per un anno

IN NOME DI SUA MAESTÀ
VITTORIO EMANUELE III
PER GRAZIA DI DIO E PER VOLONTÀ DELLA NAZIONE
RE D'ITALIA.

PASSAPORTO

...sciato a *Sovino Angelo*

...o *fu Francesco*

...lla *di Brunone Teresa*

...a *S. Vitaliano* Prov. di *Caserta*

...*20 Giugno 1903*

...dente a *Mariglianella* Prov. di *Caserta*

...o civile *Celibe*

...essione *Bracciante*

...leggere *sì* Sa scrivere *sì*

...zione di leva ...

Passaporto *2284* N. del Registro corrispondente *1*

... Prefettura di *Nola*

"Sicula Americana„
SOCIETÀ DI NAVIGAZIONE ED IMPRESE MARITTIME

563

PASSAPORTO

Meals and Memories with Nonno

Francesco Iovine, Ashley Carr

Memories translated by
Francesca Di Matteo

gatekeeper press™
Columbus, Ohio

This book is dedicated to everyone who has
their own meals and memories with a loved one.

contents

Scan here for videos of recipes

introduction

introduzione

This cookbook is to honor my grandfather, Angelo Iovine, who lived to be 101.

Like many people who live longer than a century, his extraordinary longevity had little to do with luck and everything to do with how he lived. And most importantly, how he ate. The greatest gift that Angelo brought from the Old Country was a way of cooking and a way of eating. Perhaps something that is rare today but all the more important. As he knew well, great food is not only a delight to the senses, but the foundation of a happier and healthier life.

Of course, all great food has a story. Here's my grandfather's: Angelo was born in the Mariglianella commune of Naples, Italy, in 1903. His parents, my great grandparents, were farmers. Like most farmers, they were blessed with a great deal of good sense, especially when it came to the greatest of Italian arts—cooking.

They taught Angelo that fresh, seasonal ingredients were the most important part of any dish. If you didn't make it from scratch, you didn't make it at all, and preserving and canning were paramount to a well-stocked kitchen.

Angelo came of age during a turbulent period in European history and my great grandmother didn't want to see Angelo shipped off to war. So, she shipped him off to America instead. After a sixteen day journey aboard the Guglielmo Pierce, Angelo was processed through Ellis Island on February 17, 1921. He was also among one of the last immigrants who passed through Ellis Island. Partially due to continued troubles in Europe and partially because of my grandmother's health, Angelo was never able to set foot on Italian soil again.

But Angelo's life was just getting started. He quickly assimilated to New York City and went to work on a trolley car for the Department of Transportation before settling into a long career with the Parks Department. Along the way, he met and married my grandmother, Rose. She was born right here in New York but her parents were from the same commune as my Nonno's family in Naples, where he grew up. That wasn't exactly luck either.

Despite being thousands of miles from home, he never forgot the culinary lessons imparted by his parents. He made everything from scratch—using fresh, seasonal ingredients. He canned, he preserved, and he kept this balanced, Mediterranean diet central to his life, with recipes you'll find in this book.

Dedico questo libro a mio nonno Angelo Iovine, che visse fino a 101 anni.

Come per molti degli ultracentenari, la sua straordinaria longevità ebbe ben poco a che vedere con la fortuna. Piuttosto, fu proprio il suo stile di vita—la sua alimentazione, soprattutto—a regalargli quei preziosi anni in più.

Il più grande regalo che nonno Angelo portò con sé dal vecchio continente fu un nuovo modo di cucinare e un nuovo modo di mangiare, al giorno d'oggi forse poco considerato, ma di fondamentale importanza. Come lui ben sapeva, seguire una buona alimentazione non è solamente una delizia per i sensi, bensì la base di una vita felice e salutare.

Ogni buona cucina porta con sé una grande storia. Questa è quella di nonno Angelo.

Angelo nacque nel 1903 a Mariglianella, in provincia di Napoli. Da buoni contadini, i suoi genitori avevano la fortuna di possedere un eccezionale buon gusto, specialmente per quanto riguardava la più grande arte italiana: la cucina.

Con il passare degli anni, apprese da loro che la parte più importante di ogni piatto erano proprio gli ingredienti, freschissimi e di stagione, e che le pietanze dovevano essere create partendo da zero.

Gli insegnarono inoltre che il confezionamento e la conservazione dei prodotti creati erano le fondamenta di una cucina ben fornita.

Divenne maggiorenne durante un periodo molto turbolento della storia europea. La mia bisnonna non ne voleva sapere di vedere suo figlio spedito in guerra, quindi decise piuttosto di spedirlo in America. Dopo un viaggio di sedici giorni a bordo della nave Guglielmo Peirce, Angelo venne registrato a Ellis Island il 17 febbraio del 1921, tra gli ultimi immigrati a sbarcare sull'isola. In parte a causa dei continui tumulti in Europa, in parte a causa della malattia di sua moglie, non fece mai più ritorno in Italia.

La sua vita, tuttavia, era appena agli inizi. Fu presto assorbito da New York City e cominciò a lavorare come conducente di tram per il Dipartimento dei Trasporti, prima di lanciarsi in una lunga e ambiziosa carriera nel Dipartimento dei Parchi Urbani.

Strada facendo, incontrò e sposò mia nonna Rose, nata a New York ma con i genitori proprio della stessa cittadina in provincia di Napoli, Mariglianella, dove Angelo trascorse l'infanzia. Coincidenze?

Nonostante la vita a migliaia di chilometri da casa, Angelo non ripose mai nel cassetto le lezioni culinarie dispensate dai suoi genitori. Creò tutto da zero, utilizzando solo ingredienti freschissimi e di stagione. Confezionava e conservava i frutti delle sue mani e manteneva la cara e vecchia dieta mediterranea al centro della sua vita, con le ricette che troverai in questo libro.

He ate mostly pasta and vegetables and only ate meat once or twice a week, whatever was left-over from Sunday dinner. At the time, this was also known as "the poor man's diet" because meat was expensive, as it still is. Call it what you want, my grandfather's cooking was so good, you could smell it from the driveway.

Angelo's philosophy on food was to keep it fresh and keep it simple. He taught me that cooking should be about creating and enjoying the process. Don't overcomplicate things when you don't need to, and just have fun.

Was my grandfather's diet the sole reason he lived such a long and exemplary life, as he maintained? It's hard to say. But personally, I'm not going to argue with a man who was born before the Model T was invented and lived long enough to see the launch of Facebook.

These recipes are what my Nonno would eat in a basic week, a glimpse into his cooking routine. These include his daily coffee, Sunday gravy, simple salads to more complex dishes, but nothing beyond your capability to prepare.

So, whether you're looking to lose weight, improve your health, or simply take your cooking to the next level, I invite you to try these Iovine family recipes—born of the Italian countryside, lovingly carried across the ocean and perfected right here in New York City.

Most importantly, it is not about what the final product looks like. Maybe your final dish won't be pretty or won't be trending on Instagram or whatever, but that doesn't matter. Life isn't picture-perfect, nor is our cooking!

What matters the most is the smiles the food brings to the table and the memories made.

Buon appetito!
Francesco Iovine

Nonno's favorite bird was a cardinal and it's said that when a cardinal appears to you in nature, it's representing a loved one who has passed on. You'll notice the cardinal throughout this book for that special reason.

Consumava soprattutto pasta e verdure; la carne solo una o due volte a settimana, quello che avanzava dal pranzo della domenica. A quell'epoca, la dieta mediterranea era conosciuta come "dieta pove-ra", poiché la carne era considerata molto cara, come lo è tuttora. Chiamatela come volete, ma la cucina di mio nonno era buona, ma così buona che riuscivi a sentirne il profumo fin dalla strada, ancora prima di metter piede in casa.

Le parole chiave della sua filosofia di cucina erano due: semplicità e freschezza. Nient'altro. Mi insegnò che cucinare significa creare e amarne il processo, non rendere complicate le cose quando non è necessario e, semplicemente, divertirsi.

Che sia stata la sua alimentazione l'unica ragi-one per cui visse una vita così lunga ed esemplare? Difficile a dirsi, ma non mi sento di contrastare il pensiero di un uomo che nacque prima dell'inven-zione della Ford Model T e visse così a lungo da testimoniare il lancio di Facebook.

Le ricette che troverete sono le pietanze che mio nonno era solito consumare durante una settimana normale, un assaggio della sua routine culinaria: il suo caffè quotidiano, il sugo della domenica, semplici insalate e piatti più elaborati, ma niente di difficile da preparare.

Che tu stia cercando di perdere peso, migliorare la tua salute o semplicemente far fare un salto di qualità alle tue abilità culinarie, ti invito a provare le ricette della famiglia Iovine, nate nella campagna italiana, amorevolmente trasportate da una parte all'altra dell'oceano e perfezionate proprio qui, a New York City.

Vorrei lasciarti un ultimo consiglio: non preoccuparti di creare piatti esteticamente belli da vedere. Magari il risultato finale non sarà così perfetto da diventare di tendenza su Instagram, ma non è quello che conta. La vita—e tanto meno quello che cuciniamo—non è una fotografia perfetta.

Quello che conta davvero è il sorriso che il cibo fa spuntare sulle labbra di chi è seduto al tavolo, e i ricordi che creerà per sempre.

Buon appetito!
Francesco Iovine

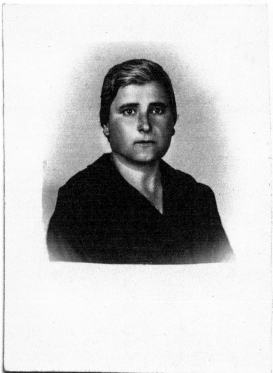

12   Nonno's sister Rachele   › Nonno's zia Vincenzina and cousins

The pots my family had (and some that you will need for recipes in this book) were the following:

A pot big enough to boil 2 lbs of
  pasta
Pots to hold 4–8 quarts of liquid
Two frying pans, of 8 inches and
  12 inches diameter
A black and white speckle roasting
  pan 12x17 in
A black and white speckle
covered roasting pan 8x12 in
A baking pan 9x13 in
Square baking sheet pans
rolling pin
a pastry cutter tool
Measuring cups & Spoons

Nonno's pantry

These items were always in my grandfather's pantry.

Olive oil (for frying)
Extra Virgin Olive Oil
Garlic
Locatelli pecorino Romano
  (aka Grating cheese)
Imported provolone
Blue cheese gorgonzola
Green & black olives
Home canned tomatoes, crushed
  tomatoes and tomato paste
  (with these three items he
  could create the desired sauce
  for the dish he was preparing)
Dried sausage or sopressata,
  hot & sweet
Di Lusso Genoa salame
  (unsliced; 2–3 pieces he would
  slice himself)
Assorted Pastas cooked to
  the directions on package

Nonno's market

Nonno was very in tune with his vegetables and fruit and went shopping two–three times a week, not letting the fact that he was unable to drive stop him. Either he walked or someone in the family drove him, so he could get the freshest produce. His two favorite locations to shop were Cross Island Fruits in Lynbrook for fruit and vegetables and Sansone Market in Garden City (info at page 142).

Nonno also shopped at his local supermarket called Village Market that has been owned by the Nargentino family for over 40 years.

Nonno's meal plan

Nonno was very understanding of life and believed that moderation was key in all things. He would buy all the ingredients to make meatballs on Friday, leaving 2–3 out for Sunday Gravy and the rest were frozen and taken out as needed for Sunday Gravy. He did the same thing with eggplant. The sausages were also portioned to two per serving and frozen to use later. He also had the same breakfast (È Mort) and fruit every day.

Visit the website *mealsandmemorieswithnonno.com* for an example of Nonno's weekly meal plan.

For our vegetarian and vegan friends—many of these recipes can be made without meat or animal products
and can be swapped with vegan ingredients!

‹ Nonno's courtyard in Mariglianella   ˆ Nonno Angelo's brother-in-law Vincenzo and his nephew Saverio; niece Raffaella; Maria and Raffaella; Gennarino, Carlo, Vincenzo and Saverio.

These photos were sent to Nonno from his nieces, nephews and friends saying "Ciao!"

This was Nonno's version of social media and the only bits of home that he ever got to see again.

Ellis Island

On February 2, 1921, at the young age of 17, Nonno left the port of Naples on the Guglielmo Peirce to set out on his quest for a new life in the United States of America.

His mother was intent on her son being able to have a better life than he could in Italy, even though she knew it meant she would most likely never see him in person again. Nonno never spoke about this with us nor did we ever ask so I've thought a lot of how he must've felt during this time. Truly, I think deep down he knew that was the final time he'd be able hug his mother and feel the warmth of her embrace and the smell of her soap on her skin. I doubt he ever forgot what that moment felt like.

The journey onboard the "Steerge," better known as third-class, took two weeks to get to Ellis Island. The environment for third-class passengers has been described by historians as crowded, unsanitary and located near the bottom of the steamships. Just imagine the stench, heat, and darkness these immigrants sat in while their hopes and fears crashed inside of them like the waves of the Atlantic Ocean they were crossing, causing many of them to get terrible sea sickness.

I think of my Nonno at 17 years old, surrounded by strangers, in a place he didn't know, going somewhere he's never been, and leaving behind the only life that he's ever experienced. He must've had thoughts and "what-ifs" overflowing his mind all the while having to remain focused and strong. Knowing Nonno the way I did, I imagined he kept quiet, minded his business and turned to the only thing that he still had which was familiar to him; God. I think he felt when he prayed, he was also speaking to his mother and that brought him comfort in those balmy and congested bunks on the ship.

On February 17, 1921, Nonno finally arrived in the New York Harbor. After docking, Nonno had to take a ferry over to Ellis Island with the other third-class passengers who were required to have a thorough and detailed inspection upon arriving in New York. First and second-class passengers were able to skip this step and have a brief inspection before getting onboard originally.

Il 2 febbraio del 1921, alla giovane età di 17 anni, nonno Angelo lasciò il porto di Napoli a bordo della Guglielmo Peirce per partire alla ricerca di una nuova vita negli Stati Uniti D'America.

Sua madre aveva preso questa decisione con il profondo desiderio che suo figlio potesse riuscire ad avere una vita migliore di quella alla quale era destinato in Italia, nonostante fosse ben consapevole del fatto che, probabilmente, ciò avrebbe significato non rivederlo mai più. Il nonno non ci disse mai— e noi osammo mai chiedere—cos'avesse provato davvero in quel periodo della sua vita; penso che in cuor suo sapesse che si trattava dell'ultima volta in cui avrebbe potuto avere sua mamma così vicina, sentire il calore del suo abbraccio e il profumo del suo sapone sulla pelle. Dubito che abbia mai dimenticato la sensazione di quel preciso istante.

Dopo due settimane di viaggio nella "Steerge", ovvero la terza classe, la nave attraccò a Ellis Island. Lo spazio dei passeggeri di terza classe, localizzato vicino al fondo del piroscafo, fu descritto dagli storici come molto affollato e antigienico. Immagina il fetore, il caldo e l'oscurità in cui sedevano gli immigrati, mentre speranze e paure si infrangevano dentro di loro come le onde dell'Oceano Atlantico che stavano attraversando, e che provocavano a molti un terribile mal di mare.

Penso a mio nonno con i suoi 17 anni, circondato da estranei, in un posto che non conosceva, in direzione di un luogo che per lui era ancora un'incognita e con alle spalle l'unica vita che conosceva davvero. Immagino gli innumerevoli pensieri e i vari "cosa succederà se…" che gli attraversavano la mente, il tutto sforzandosi di rimanere forte e determinato.

Per come conoscevo io il nonno, me lo immagino taciturno, concentrato su sé stesso e con i pensieri rivolti a ciò che di più familiare gli fosse rimasto: Dio. Immagino che, pregando, si sentisse vicino anche a sua madre, e questo era ciò che gli donava conforto in quelle cuccette fredde e strette della nave.

Il 17 febbraio del 1921, nonno Angelo sbarcò finalmente nel porto di New York. Dopo l'attracco, tutti i passeggeri di terza classe dovevano prendere un traghetto per Ellis Island, dove sarebbero stati

Once Nonno's inspection was complete, he was able to set out and create the life for himself that his mother dreamed of. As Nonno stood with Lady Liberty at his back, he realized that the past two weeks were only the very first steps of his journey that lay ahead. It's as if the aspiration and ambition flowed from the East River right into Nonno's veins as he took his first steps into the Big Apple.

The below is an excerpt from an article titled "Sailing to the Land of Liberty":

> Most immigrants entered the United States through New York Harbor, although there were other ports of entry in cities such as Boston, Philadelphia, Baltimore, San Francisco, and New Orleans. The great steamship companies like the White Star, Red Star, Cunard, and Hamburg-America Lines played a significant role in the history of Ellis Island and immigration as a whole.
>
> First and second class passengers arriving in New York Harbor were not required to undergo the inspection process at Ellis Island. Instead, these passengers received a cursory inspection aboard the ship; theory being that if a person could afford to purchase a first or second class ticket they were affluent and less likely to become a public charge in America due to medical or legal reasons. However, regardless of class, sick passengers or those with legal problems were sent to Ellis Island for further inspection.

For the full article and more information about Ellis Island, visit *EllisIsland.org*

sottoposti ad un'ispezione completa e dettagliata prima dell'arrivo nella metropoli. I passeggeri di prima e seconda classe potevano saltare questo passaggio, a loro era riservato solamente un breve controllo ancor prima di salire a bordo nel luogo di partenza.

Conclusa l'ispezione, era finalmente giunto il momento di iniziare a creare la nuova vita che sua madre aveva tanto sognato per lui. Con la Statua della Libertà alle spalle, si rese conto che le ultime due settimane trascorse in nave non erano altro che i primissimi passi del grande e ignoto viaggio che aveva davanti. Mentre si avvicinava alla Grande Mela, era come se ambizione e desideri fluissero dalle acque dell'East River e arrivassero a scorrere direttamente nelle sue vene.

Segue un estratto da un articolo intitolato "Navigando verso la Terra della Libertà":

> La maggior parte degli immigrati arrivava negli Stati Uniti attraverso il porto di New York, sebbene vi fossero diversi porti di ingresso in città come Boston, Filadelfia, Baltimora, San Francisco e New Orleans. Le grandi compagnie di navi a vapore come la White Start, la Cunard e la Hamburg-America Lines ebbero un ruolo significativo nella storia di Ellis Island e del fenomeno dell'immigrazione in generale.
>
> I passeggeri di prima e seconda classe in arrivo al porto di New York non erano tenuti a sottoporsi al processo di ispezione a Ellis Island; ricevevano solamente un controllo molto superficiale una volta arrivati a bordo della nave. La spiegazione più diffusa a proposito è che, se una persona poteva permettersi di acquistare un biglietto di prima o seconda classe, ciò significava che era benestante e quindi non sarebbe probabilmente diventata un onere pubblico in America per ragioni mediche o legali. Tuttavia, indipendentemente dalla classe, i passeggeri malati o con problemi legali venivano inviati a Ellis Island per un'ispezione approfondita.

Per leggere l'articolo completo e per avere ulteriori informazioni su Ellis Island, vi invito a visitare la pagina *EllisIsland.org*

S. S. "GUGLIELMO PEIRCE" Passengers

No. on List	HEAD-TAX STATUS (This column for use of Government officials only.)	NAME IN FULL		Age		Sex	Married or single	Calling or occupation	Able to—	
		Family name.	Given name.	Yrs.	Mos.				Read.	Read what language [or, if exemption claimed, on what ground].
1			ANTONIO							
2		ZENOBIO	GIUSEPPE	20		M	S	Tailor	yes	4-4623 italian
3		MALLOZZI	ANTONIO	17		M	S	Laborer	yes	4-4623 italian
4		MALLOZZI	TOMMASO	16		M	S	Laborer	yes	4-4623 italian
5		FORTUNA	GIOVANNI	16		M	S	Laborer	yes	4-4623 italian
6		CAMEROTA	SEBASTIANO	16		M	S	Laborer	yes	4-2623 italian
7		ALBANO	ANGELA	22		F	S		yes	4-673 italian
8		FRATE	MICHELE	18		M	S	Laborer	yes	4-2675 italian
9		CONTE	MARIANO	22		M	M	Laborer	yes	4-4623 italian
10		GRELLA	CARMINE	25		M	S	Farmlab.	yes	4-4623 italian
11		ZENOBIO	GIOVANNI	20		M	S	Laborer	yes	4-4623 italian
12		CORRENTE	LUCIA	22		F	S	Housekeep.	yes	4-2673 italian
13		DI PIETRO						Laborer		italian
14	*	ANDRETTI	ANGELO	16		M	S	Laborer	yes	italian
15		LAIMITTI	NICOLA	20		M	S	Laborer	yes	4-4623 italian
16		MASONE	GIUSEPPE	41		M	M	Laborer	yes	4-4623 italian
17		MALLOZZI	TOMMASO	16		M	S	Laborer	yes	4-623 italian
18		MELE	ANNUNZIATA	19		F	S	Laborer	yes	italian
19		IMPROTA	SALVATORE	17		M	S	Laborer	yes	4-4623 italian
20		CAMEROTA	ANGELO	25		M	M	Laborer	yes	4-2623 italian
21		CONTE	PASQUALE	24		M	M	Laborer	yes	4-4623 italian
22		LOMBARDI	FRANCESCO	24		M	S	Laborer	yes	4-623 italian
23		MORLANDO	FILIPPO	32		M	M	shoemak.	yes	4-4623 italian
24		CARPINO	ADRIANO	23		M	S	Laborer	yes	4-2623 italian
25		TRAMONTANO	ANTONIO	17		M	S	Farmlab.	yes	4-4623 italian
26		JOVINE	ANGELO	17		M	S	Laborer	yes	4-4623 italian
27		PRINCIPATO	GIOVANNI	15		M	S	shoemak.	yes	italian
28		PRINCIPATO	CARMELA	15		F	S	Farmlab.	yes	4-673 italian
29		TRAMONTANO	ANTONIO	40		M	M	Farmlab.	yes	4-4623 italian
30			SALVATORE						yes	italian

Lewis C. Marsh 3/2/21

Total passengers 29
U. S. citizens . . . . .
Aliens 29

PID:100139010510

F ALIEN PASSENGERS FOR THE UNITED

United States, and all aliens arriving at a port of said insular possessions from a foreign port, a port of continental United

This (white) sheet is for the listing of

NAPLES _____, 2 FEB 1921 _____, 191

10	11		12	13	
	*Last permanent residence.		The name and complete address of nearest relative or friend in country whence alien came.	Final destination. (* Intended future permanent residence.)	
Race or people.	Country.	City or town.		State.	City or town.
					SCRANTON
ITALIAN SO.	ITALY	MINTURNO	Father Zonobio Filippo – Minturno	N.Y.	LITTLE FALLS
ITALIAN SO.	ITALY	MINTURNO	Father Mallozzi Giuseppe – Minturno	Conn.	STANFORD
ITALIAN SO.	ITALY	MINTURNO	Father Mallozzi Angelo – Minturno	Mass.	WESTON
ITALIAN SO.	ITALY	MINTURNO	Mother D'Arienzo Maria – Minturno	Pa.	SCRANTON
ITALIAN SO.	ITALY	MINTURNO	Mother Comerota Adamo – Minturno	Pa.	ROCHESTER
ITALIAN SO.	ITALY	MINTURNO	Parents: Albano Giovanni and Tuccia Fona Maria – Minturno	Pa.	ROCHESTER
ITALIAN SO.	ITALY	MINTURNO	Mother Cardillo Maria – Minturno	N.Y.	ENDICOTT
ITALIAN SO.	ITALY	MINTURNO	Wife Sparagna Vittoria – Minturno	Pa.	ROCHESTER
ITALIAN SO.	ITALY	MINTURNO	Father Grolla Nicola – Minturno	Pa.	PHILADELPHIA
ITALIAN SO.	ITALY	MINTURNO	Parents: Zonobio Pasquale and Bisco Maria – Minturno	Ohio	BARSETON
ITALIAN SO.	ITALY	MINTURNO	Father Corrente Pasquale – Minturno	N.Y.	UTICA
ITALIAN SO.	ITALY	MINTURNO	Colomba – Minturno	Conn.	BRIDGEPORT
ITALIAN SO.	ITALY	MINTURNO	Mother Di Girolamo Giuseppa – Minturno	Pa.	PHILADELPHIA
ITALIAN SO.	ITALY	MINTURNO	Father Junnitti Pasquale – Minturno	Pa.	ROCHESTER
ITALIAN SO.	ITALY	MINTURNO	Wife Sciarretta Concetta – Minturno	Conn.	BRIDGEPORT
ITALIAN SO.	ITALY	MINTURNO	Parents: Mallozzi Angelo and Tartaglia Rosa – Minturno	N.J.	ELIZABETH
ITALIAN SO.	ITALY	MINTURNO	Brother Melo Pacifico – Minturno	Pa.	SCRANTON
ITALIAN SO.	ITALY	MINTURNO	Father Improta Antonio – Minturno	Conn.	STANFORD
ITALIAN SO.	ITALY	MINTURNO	Wife Granato Elisabetta – Minturno	Mass.	WALTHAM
ITALIAN SO.	ITALY	MINTURNO	Wife Forte Marta – Minturno	Pa.	ROCHESTER
ITALIAN SO.	ITALY	MINTURNO	Father Lombardi Gaetano – Minturno	Md.	SO. CUMBERLAND
ITALIAN SO.	ITALY	MINTURNO	Wife Mallozzi Anna – Minturno	Pa.	WASHINGTON
ITALIAN SO.	ITALY	MARIGLIANELLA	Parents: Carpino Giovanni and Jovine Morianna – Mariglianella	Pa.	BRADDOCK
ITALIAN SO.	ITALY	CASTEL CISTERNA	Parents: Tremontano Pietro and Menachino Felicia – Castel Cisterna	N.Y.	BROOKLYN
ITALIAN SO.	ITALY	MARIGLIANELLA	Mother Sommese Teresa – Mariglianella	N.Y.	JAMAICA
ITALIAN SO.	ITALY	MARIGLIANELLA	Mother Provvisiero Saveria – Mariglianella	N.Y.	JAMAICA
ITALIAN SO.	ITALY	MARIGLIANELLA	Mother Corbicioro Saveria – Mariglianella	N.Y.	JAMAICA
ITALIAN SO.	ITALY	CASTEL CISTERNA	Wife Jannelli Maria – Castel Cisterna	N.Y.	BROOKLYN
ITALIAN SO.	ITALY	MARIGLIANELLA		N.Y.	JAMAICA

* Permanent residence within the meaning of this manifest shall be actual or intended residence of one year or more.
† List of races will be found on the back of this sheet.

✓ Jovine, Angelo

Nonno's breakfast
E'Mort

Here's a little joke for your morning coffee in the words of Nonno: "Why do priests eat cantaloupe melons and husbands eat honeydew melons? Why you ask?? Because priests can't elope and husbands have a honey-do list!"

You will need:
coffee from the day before
milk
sugar
biscotto or stale Italian bread

Nonno's tip:
Warm this up on the stove, not the microwave!

The meaning of "è mort" is "the dead coffee from yesterday."

Take old coffee and warm it up.

Add biscotto* or stale Italian bread.

Add milk and sugar.

* It's important to note that the biscotto that Nonno used was called pane biscotto, which translates to twice baked bread, not to be confused with the biscotti you may see at the store that's dipped in chocolate or loaded with sugar-filled ingredients. If you don't have twice baked bread, you can use stale bread or fresh bread in its place.

Beans are undoubtedly one of the most popular dish choices for people across the world, from every kind of culture. Sure, you can use canned beans but nothing is more authentic than the old fashioned dry beans that you prepare yourself. Follow these easy steps to cook your own beans or chickpeas for any recipe that calls for them.

Take 1–2 cups of beans or chickpeas and place in a 4 quart pot.

Fill ¾ of the pot with water and bring to a boil.

Leave cover askew and let boil for approximately 10 minutes.

After 10 minutes, turn off heat and fully cover the pot with the lid.

Let sit for a minimum of 1 hour. Nonno would cook the beans or chickpeas in the morning to use in the afternoon.

Drain off old liquid and add fresh water until the pot is ¾ full.

Cook until desired texture, usually between 20–40 minutes depending on how long they soaked.

Please note: this is not for smaller beans (i.e., navy beans).

› Nonno's sister Rachele and brother-in-law Vincenzo with their children

Warm white bean salad
insalata calda di fagioli bianchi

You will need:
2 cups cannelloni beans
4 cloves garlic (sliced or chopped)
extra virgin olive oil
  (4–6 second pour)
½–1 juice of a lemon, depending
  on the level of lemon you like
  and the size of the lemon
salt to taste
pinch of oregano to taste

Nonno's tip:
Good to make a large batch of
these to use in different recipes.

Cook beans to desired texture—
between al dente and full
(see page 24).

While beans are hot, stir in garlic
and 3 second pour of EVOO.

Transfer into serving bowl and
drizzle with the rest of EVOO,
lemon juice, salt, and a pinch of
oregano last.

August salad
insalata di agosto

You will need:
3–4 boiled potatoes (quartered)
3–4 fresh tomatoes (quartered)
2 bell peppers (sliced)
2 red onions (sliced)
2 cucumbers (cut)
1 teaspoon oregano
extra virgin olive oil (⅛ cup)
1–2 liters of water

Required pans:
1 large glass bowl

Nonno's tip:
All of these vegetables and herbs
would've been found in my garden.
Try growing something of your
own—even if it's an oregano plant!

Add all the vegetables into bowl
and mix.

Fill bowl ¼ to ½ way up the
vegetables with water.

Add salt, oregano and EVOO and
mix again.

Serve with crusty Italian bread
for the true Mediterranean
experience.

AUGUST - SALAD - IS - MADE - O[N]
THE - DAY - BEFORE - THE ASSUMPTION - ON
AUG. 14TH, CONSISTS - OF - BOILED - POTATOES - C[UT]
AND - PEELED - TOMATOES - CUT - 1 - GREEN -
SWEET - PEPPER - 2 - RED - ONIONS - CUT - UP
1 CUCUMBER - CUT UP - THEN - ADD - SOME - OIL
SALT + OREGANO - SPICES - A. LITTLE - BIT
OF - WATER - THEN - MIX - IT - ALL - UP - + SERV[E]
WE - ALSO - HAVE - FOR - DESERRT

HONEYDEW - MELON

MARCH - 19 - IS - ST. JOSEPH - DA[Y]
WE - HAVE - ITALIAN - CAKE - THEY - CALL - THEM
ZEPPALA - COOKIES

WE HAVE - FARINA - CAKE - ONE - DAY
BEFORE - LENT - STARTS

1/2 BOX FARINA - SMALL - BOX - (350 DEGR.
OVEN
USE - 2 QUARTS - MILK - WHEN - IT - COMES - TO - A - BOIL
PUT - FARINA - IN - A - LITTLE - AT - THE - TIME - AND
STIR - GOOD - NO - LUMPS THEN - ADD TWO - CUPS - O[F]
SUGAR + 1/4 LB. BUTTER - WHEN - COOLED - OFF - ADD
1 DOZ. EGGS - AND - SKINS - OF - 2 TANGERINES - CUT

Green salad
insalata verde

You will need:
**romaine, boston or greenleaf
 lettuce**
garlic (2–3 cloves, sliced)
**extra virgin olive oil
 (3–4 second pour)**
vinegar (red or white)
½ onion (sliced; optional)
lemon (optional, if in season)
pinch of salt

Required pots:
1 mixing bowl

Nonno's tip:
I never bought iceberg lettuce in
my life. It was whatever was on sale
that made its way into my house!

Wash and dry lettuce then place in
a bowl.

Add salt and mix, then add garlic
and onion.

Add EVOO and vinegar or fresh
lemon for dressing.

This dish was always served at the
end of the meal, never as a starter.

Nonna Rose's mother Rachele and father Antonio

Artichokes
carciofi

This dish is called "Carciofo alla Rachele" in my family because when my daughter Rachele was a baby her delicate and powerful cry sounded like the squeak the artichoke made when making this dish. Since then, I've always loved that sound!

Questo piatto è chiamato "Carciofo alla Rachele" dalla mia famiglia, perchè, quando mia figlia Rachele era piccola, il suo pianto delicato e forte allo stesso tempo sembrava il suono che fa il carciofo quando si prepara questo piatto. Da allora, ho sempre amato questo suono!

You will need:
2–6 artichokes
garlic (6–8 cloves)
1 head of fresh parsley
¼ cup grating cheese
a good pinch of salt per artichoke
extra virgin olive oil (3 second pour for each artichoke)
water

Required pots:
1 large pot

Nonno's tip:
Be careful of artichoke's pointy tips while handling them, as they can hurt!

Cut off artichoke's stems, leaving a flat surface on the bottom.

Cut/peel away the outer layer of skin on the artichoke stem. (See video how to prepare an artichoke on our website *mealsandmemorieswithnonno.com*)

Place artichoke top down on the counter, put your hand in the area you just cut and push down—it will make a squeaking sound.

Place artichokes cut side down, spread leaves apart and start stuffing garlic, grated cheese and parsley sporadically between the leaves working from outside to the center. Sprinkle with salt.

In a large pot, place each artichoke so they're top up (it may be a tight squeeze).

Pour EVOO over each artichoke for 3 seconds then add water until it's just over half way up the artichoke. Cover and bring to boil.

Once boiling, bring to a medium/low simmer. Check water often until it's about ½ of what you started with. Now maintain that level by adding water as needed.

Cook artichokes for 1–2 hours. The more they cook, the tenderer they will be.

Store in a glass container.

Lima bean soup
zuppa di fagioli di Lima

You will need:
1 cup lima beans
2 stalks celery (sliced)
2 cloves garlic (whole or
  quartered)
3–4 cups of water
extra virgin olive oil
  (2 second pour)
pinch of salt
pinch of oregano

Required pots:
6 quart pot

Nonno's tips:
Adding fresh bread with this zuppa
is a good way to heft it up.

In 6 quart pot, add 3 cups of water and lima beans and bring to a boil.

Once boiling, add celery, garlic and oregano.

When beans are ½ way cooked, add the EVOO and salt and continue cooking until beans are tender.

Escarole & beans soup
zuppa di scarole e fagioli

You will need:
1 large head of escarole
garlic (6–8 cloves; sliced,
chopped or halved)
1 onion (sliced)
2–3 cups cooked beans (reserve
the liquid)
extra virgin olive oil
(6–8 second pour)
1–2 liters of water

Required pots:
1 large pot

Nonno's tip:
Like many of my other recipes,
this dish can be served as a main
course or a side.

Wash and rinse escarole thoroughly
and place leaves in a large pot.

Add onion, garlic and salt on top
but do not mix yet.

Add 1 liter of water so it's over ¼
of the pot and then add EVOO.

Cover and cook on medium-high
heat until escarole becomes soft.
Stir occasionally for approximately
20 minutes for the escarole
to soften and bring down to a
simmer, adding more water
if necessary.

Add beans and their liquid (the
amount of liquid is based on what
you're serving).

Stir until desired texture is reached
(Nonno preferred soft, so 1–1½
hours).

Enjoy with good crusty bread,
cheese and salami!

employment

Nonno had a wonderful work ethic. His first big job in the United States was with the City of New York for the Trolley Car in the Department of Transportation. In that time, around 1922, the trolley system had about 500 miles of tracks and carried a billion passengers a year. That's about the same amount of tracks as the current subway systems, only NYC has several million more residents now. It was a thriving business and created a pathway for many people like Nonno who ended up being employed by the city of New York until he retired.

He moved on to the Department of Water and Sewers to which he put in the necessary time to get transferred to the Parks and Rec Department. At that time, when you worked for the city, you could transfer within departments rather easily so Nonno took the opportunity to do so.

In the Parks Department, he was totally in his element being surrounded by plants and wildlife. He got to meet all types of like-minded people who loved nature and the outdoors the same way he did. In fact, he was at work for the Parks Department when he learned how to grow watercress from people who were planting it. He genuinely looked forward to going to work every day because it was always a chance to learn something or simply make a human connection.

Nonno eventually retired (in 1968) but, as displayed throughout this book, he never really stopped working. He was a true example of someone who loved what they did for a living and that it could provide for his family. You could say that Nonno really achieved the American Dream.

Nonno Angelo ebbe sempre una grande etica del lavoro; il suo primo vero impiego negli Stati Uniti è stato quello di conducente di tram per il Dipartimento dei Trasporti della città di New York. A quel tempo, intorno al 1922, il sistema tranviario della metropoli includeva circa 900 km di binari e trasportava un miliardo di passeggeri all'anno; si tratta pressappoco della stessa quantità di binari dell'attuale metropolitana, ma rispetto ad allora New York oggi ha diversi milioni di residenti in più. Si trattava di un'attività in crescita, che permise di costruire una carriera lavorativa a molte persone come il nonno, che rimase impiegato della città di New York fino alla pensione.

Fu trasferito in seguito al Dipartimento delle Acque e delle Fognature, nel quale rimase il tempo necessario per poter passare al Dipartimento dei Parchi Urbani. Allora, quando lavoravi per la città avevi la possibilità di trasferirti all'interno di diversi dipartimenti piuttosto facilmente, motivo per il quale il nonno lavorò in diversi ambiti.

Il dipartimento che più lo rappresentava era quello dei Parchi Urbani: era continuamente circondato da piante e fauna selvatica e aveva modo di incontrare colleghi che, proprio come lui, amavano la natura e la vita all'aria aperta. Fu proprio durante quel periodo, infatti, che imparò a coltivare il crescione osservando alcune persone che lo piantavano. Ogni giorno non vedeva l'ora di andare al lavoro, perché per lui era sempre un'occasione per imparare qualcosa, o semplicemente per tessere nuove relazioni.

Nonostante l'inevitabile raggiungimento della pensione ad un certo punto della vita, come si evince dai racconti il nonno non smise mai veramente di lavorare. Era un vero esempio di una persona che amava ciò che faceva per vivere e per poter provvedere ai bisogni della famiglia. Possiamo dire che nonno Angelo realizzò davvero il "sogno americano".

30-2001-29 I. S. Form 24

Application No. . . . .   Received . . . .

LABOR CLASS
MUNICIPAL CIVIL SERVICE COMMISSION
Municipal Building, 14th Floor, Centre and Chambers Streets
Use Elevators Numbers 1 to 16 (North End of Building)
ENTRANCE ON DUANE STREET

Application for Position of *Track Repairer (Trolley Operation*

APPLICANTS FOR POSITIONS IN DEPT. OF STREET CLEANING MUST PRODUCE PROOF OF DATE OF BIRTH AT TIME OF FILING APPLICATION

1. What is your full name? *Angelo Covnic*
2. Where do you live? *150-16-107ax Jamaica* Borough of *Queens*
   (If you live in the Borough of Queens or Richmond, specify name of town.)
3. How long have you resided in New York State? *8 years*; in New York City *8 years*
4. Age *26*; Date of Birth *June 21 03*; Place of Birth *Italy*
5. Are you single, married, divorced or widowed? *Single*
   If married, divorced or widowed, give place of birth of husband or wife ..... Date of marriage .....
6. If not a citizen by birth, when and where were you naturalized? Date *3-4 1927* Court *Supreme L I City*
   Naturalized citizens must present their own, parent's or husband's papers when filing this application.
7. What have been your previous occupations? *Track Repairer etc*
8. By whom { were you last / are you now } employed? *Jamaica Central R R Co*
9. What { was / is } your employer's address? *N Y Blvd + Tower Pl Jamaica*
10. How long have you been doing the kind of work for which you now apply? *5-yrs*
11. Were you ever in the service of the City of New York? Ans. (Yes or No) *No*
    (If yes, state cause of leaving) .....
12. Are the answers to the above questions in your handwriting? Ans. (Yes or No) *No McCormick*
    If no, give name, address, and occupation of person who filled in application
    140-17-South St Jamaica Surveyor
13. Are you a veteran of the Civil War? Ans. (Yes or No) *No* If yes, produce discharge
14. Are you receiving a pension from the City of New York? Ans. (Yes or No) *No*
    If yes, state what Pension or Retirement Fund .....
15. Have you ever been arrested, arraigned, or summoned in a criminal court? Ans. (Yes or No) *No*
    If yes, state facts briefly .....

THIS OATH MUST BE TAKEN BEFORE A JUSTICE, NOTARY, OR OTHER OFFICER COMPETENT TO ADMINISTER IT.

County of .... State of ...., ss.:

I hereby swear that I have answered all the above questions truthfully; that I have signed my name, or made my mark; that I am the person to be examined; that the occupation, residence and business addresses, and other statements of each voucher as given in the voucher certificates are correct, and that each voucher is a citizen of the United States, and of good character and reputation.

{ Applicant's Signature or Mark } *α*

Sworn to before me this ....
day of .... 192 ...

NOTICE. Persons applying for positions that require previous experience must have the following certificate properly filled out by a former or present employer, showing at least one year's experience for the position applied for.

EMPLOYER'S CERTIFICATE

Date *x* ...., 192 ...

I hereby certify that .... was employed by me as a ....

for (state how long) ...., that I found him to be sober, trustworthy, industrious, and

that he is qualified for employment in the Labor Service of The City of New York. I further state that he understands the English language sufficiently well to perform the duties of said position, and that I have read the foregoing statements made by him, and believe them to be true.

Remarks : ....

Occupation .... Name ....

Business Address .... Residence ....

THESE APPLICATIONS MAY BE OBTAINED FREE OF CHARGE

[SEE OTHER SIDE]

Carpenter
Deckhand   *Driver
                  Elevator Man   Fireman (Licensed) (Stat. Fireman's
                                         Cert. Required)
                                         *Laborer

. OF HEALTH)

Lentil soup
zuppa di lenticchie

You will need:
lentils (16 oz bag)
extra virgin olive oil
  (3–4 second pour)
garlic (2 medium cloves, sliced)
1 onion (chopped)
3 carrots (unpeeled or peeled,
  rough cut)
4 stalks celery (peeled, rough cut)
bay leaf (4–6 leaves)
1 teaspoon salt
3–4 quarts water or stock of
  choice

Required pots:
1 large pot with lid

Use your sense of smell to enjoy every step of this recipe!

Sauté onion and garlic on medium heat until aromatic.

Add a pinch of salt, bay leaves, carrots and celery.

When they start to meld add lentils and wait a minute.

Add ½–¾ of water or stock, so that everything is submerged.

Bring to a boil, then reduce to simmer with lid.

Stir often and, if it gets too thick, add water.

Cook for approximately 1 hour, or longer if you want it thicker.

‹ Nonno's sister Rachele and brother-in-law Vincenzo

Chicken soup & dandelions
zuppa di pollo e denti di leone

You will need:
1 chicken (cut up)
1–2 onions (sliced)
garlic (1–2 cloves; sliced)
1 teaspoon of salt
1 bunch of dandelions

Required pots:
8 quart pot

Nonno's tip:
A large batch of this will feed you once a day for a week.

To prepare the dandelions, cut off their ends and wash thoroughly to remove sand. Once washed, blanch them by placing them in a pot of boiling water seasoned with 1 tsp salt. Let them cook on a full boil for 3–5 minutes and then drain, saving some of the water for the main dish.

Fill pot with water up to under the rivets or handles, add chicken and bring to a boil on high heat.

While waiting to boil, add onion, garlic and salt.

Once boiling, reduce to a simmer, stirring occasionally for about 30–40 minutes.

Check to see if chicken is fully cooked (meat will start to pull away from bone).

Take the breasts, legs and thighs, out of the pot, leaving the backbone in.

Let it cool so you can handle it, then remove the meat from the bone and place it back into the pot.

Add dandelions to the pot, bringing back to a boil and then lower to a simmer for 20–30 minutes. Now add some of the liquid from the dandelions to your taste.

Let cool and serve with grated cheese.

CHICKEN - SOUP - WITH - DANDELION

PUT - A - HALF - OF - A - 5 LB.
CHICKEN - cut up - TO - COOK - IN - A - POT
PUT - IN - WATER - TO - COVER
CHICKEN - AND - LET - IT - COOK simmer
UNTIL - DONE.

THEN - COOK - UP - 2 LBS OF
DANDELIONS

CLEAN - DANDELIONS + WASH
THEM - THEN - WHEN - WATER - COMES
TO - A - BOIL - COOK - DANDELIONS
UNTIL - TENDER - THEY - DO NOT
TAKE - LONG - TO - COOK. THEN - DRAIN
WATER - AND - WHEN - CHICKEN IS
COOKED - PUT - DANDELIONS - IN
THE - CHICKEN - STOCK. LET - COOK
TOGETHER - ABOUT 15 MINS. ADD
SALT. TO - TASTE

JUL • 58

Fried peppers
peperoni fritti

You will need:
**4–6 frying peppers (i.e., banana
   peppers, cubanelle peppers)**
**extra virgin olive oil
   (2–4 second pour)**
salt to taste

Optional ingredients to add:
2–3 bell peppers (sliced)
1–3 hot cherry peppers (ripped)
1–2 vinegar peppers (ripped)

This can be messy to make. Cook
peppers separately for best results.

Required pots:
1 large frying pan

Nonno's tip:
You can fry the peppers with the
seeds or without—whichever you
prefer!

In a large frying pan, heat EVOO.

Add the frying peppers and let
them start to blister, for about 7–10
minutes.*

Reduce heat and turn peppers
until soft.

Options:
a. Add eggs to the pan and cook
how you like them.

b. Put peppers into a container,
add some EVOO and let cool.

---

*   You can also start cooking
the peppers on the BBQ for raw
peppers then finish in the pan later
that day or as needed.

trolley accident

Sometime in the 1930s, Nonno was working for the Trolley Department for the City of New York which wasn't the safest job one could have in those days. He ended up falling from a trolley wire and shattered his shin. It was looking like he'd likely never be able to even walk again much less do anything else. Doctors performed a bone graft that they literally told him "had no idea if it would work or not" and Nonno didn't have much choice in the matter as there weren't other options. If he had any hope of being able to walk again, he had to take the chance.

The bone graft seemed to have been successful though and Nonno never stopped getting his exercise. He believed both physical and mental exercise was very important which is why he was consistently engaged with something. Whether he was playing checkers, lifting weights or sowing seeds—Nonno showed no sign of ever slowing down.

In the basement, aka the "cantina," there were two pulleys set up each with a rope that on one end was tied to a wooden handle and the other end was tied to window sash weights. He used this to work out with. In modern terms, this equipment would be similar to a cable machine and can be found at gyms or purchased for upwards of $2,000. It wasn't anything fancy but Nonno just used some basic materials and ingenuity to create his own device and made it work.

Despite having this traumatic event happen to him, Nonno took on every day with optimism and confidence. Fear was not something that was in his vocabulary unless of course it had to do with some kind of traditional Italian superstition. His past made him the man he was; a man that was loved very much.

Negli anni '30 nonno lavorava per il Dipartimento dei Trasporti della città di New York, non esattamente la professione più sicura che si potesse avere a quell'epoca. Difatti, purtroppo, un giorno una brutta caduta da un tram gli causò la frattura della tibia. Dai primi esami, risultò che probabilmente non sarebbe mai più stato in grado di camminare, né tantomeno di svolgere qualunque altra attività che richiedesse l'utilizzo delle gambe. I medici decisero di eseguire un trapianto osseo, nonostante ci fossero poche sicurezze sul fatto che avrebbe funzionato. Non essendoci altre opzioni, il nonno non aveva molta scelta. Se avesse voluto avere qualche minima speranza di poter tornare a camminare, avrebbe dovuto cogliere l'occasione.

Il trapianto osseo ebbe inaspettatamente successo e da quel momento nonno non smise mai di fare esercizio. Credeva fortemente che tanto l'esercizio fisico quanto quello mentale fossero di fondamentale importanza, motivo per il quale era si teneva sempre costantemente impegnato. Che stesse giocando a dama, sollevando pesi o lavorando nell'orto, non mostrava mai alcun segno di cedimento.

In cantina c'erano due barre installate ciascuna con una corda, che da un'estremità era legata ad una maniglia di legno e dall'altra ai pesi dell'anta della finestra. Questo era l'attrezzo che usava per allenarsi. Uno strumento così oggi sarebbe simile a un attrezzo multifunzionale da palestra per allenare tutto il corpo, che puoi trovare nelle palestre o comprare per circa 2000€. Non era niente di raffinato, con un po' di ingegno e del materiale semplice il nonno si era creato il suo attrezzo. Nonostante l'evento traumatico della frattura della tibia, nonno ha continuato ad affrontare ogni nuovo giorno con ottimismo e fiducia. La parola paura non era proprio presente nel suo vocabolario, a meno che, ovviamente, non avesse a che vedere con qualche superstizione della tradizione italiana. Fu il suo trascorso a renderlo l'uomo che era; un uomo molto amato.

44   Church of San Giovanni Evangelista in Mariglianella, Naples

Chickpeas with garlic & EVOO
ceci con aglio e olio d'oliva

You will need:
1 cup of dried chickpeas which
 will yield 1–½ cups
garlic (4–6 cloves; sliced)
extra virgin olive oil
 (6–8 second pour)
pinch of salt

Required pots:
1 saucepan

Nonno's tip:
These are great as a snack or
addition to another recipe.

Cook chickpeas to desired texture
(see page 24).

Warm up cooked chickpeas and
remove from heat.

Add garlic, salt, and EVOO and mix.

Broccoli rabe with garlic
broccoli rabe con aglio

You will need:
1 bunch of broccoli rabe
garlic (6–8 cloves; cut however
you prefer)
extra virgin olive oil
(4–6 second pour)
1 teaspoon of salt
water

Required pots:
1 large pot, 1 frying pan

Nonno's tip:
Blanch 2–3 heads of broccoli heads,
put into freezer bags and freeze.

In a large pot, bring water to boil.

Wash and cut ¼–½ inch of the
bottoms off of the greens.

Add salt right before add the
greens and let boil for 3–5 minutes.

Remove and drain.*

In a large frying pan, add oil, then
garlic.

Once the garlic begins to brown,
add greens (It will splatter so be
prepared!)

Enjoy with bread and cheese or a
side dish!

---

* This method is called
"blanching." You can prep this
a day before and store in the
refrigerator or frozen.

Broccoli with lemon & fresh garlic
broccoli con limone e aglio fresco

You will need:
1–2 broccoli crowns
garlic (4–6 cloves; sliced or
  chopped)
extra virgin olive oil
  (4 second pour)
juice of 1–2 lemons
pinch of salt

Nonno's tip:
The lemon in this dish will get
sourer the longer it's stored so add
the lemon right before eating for
the freshest bite.

Steam broccoli until tender. Drain
and put in a bowl.

Add garlic, salt, and EVOO and mix.

Taste and adjust salt if needed.

Add ½ a lemon's juice and
continue adding until you reach
your desired flavor.

nonno's store

My father shared with me a memory of Nonno, which I believe truly represents his personality.

Sometime in the early 1930s, before he was married and working for the trolley cars, Nonno opened a small grocery store in South Jamaica, Queens, NY, on Sutphin Blvd and Rockaway Blvd. If you don't know NYC very well, Jamaica Queens wasn't (and still isn't) exactly booming with wealth and there are a lot of families in need. Nonno knew the area and wanted to take the opportunity to open his own business.

He quickly became known around the neighborhood, as he was an outgoing guy and sincerely cared about the people who resided there. The children loved to stop by the store, because they knew Nonno would joyously give them some kind of candy or treat to enjoy. Eventually, as time went on, so did Nonno's generosity.

If someone was unable to pay the total amount for their stuff, Nonno would let them pay whatever they could afford. He ended up getting to a point where he was giving away more than he was actually selling. While this was very much kindhearted, it was also terrible for the shop's profit.

Nonno may have not been cut out to be a business owner in that sense, but I believe he had his good reasons. He empathized with these people because he'd been in their shoes before. When you come from nothing, you don't forget what it feels like and Nonno never did. His whole life, he gave whenever and wherever he could.

This giving mindset was one that carried on with him in every aspect of his life. When Nonno was given a dish of food from a neighbor or friend, the dish was always returned full with either fresh fruit from his garden or a recipe of his own. He never returned something empty and that is a great virtue.

His generosity is something that I also practice and therefore a percentage of the proceeds from this book will go to support local charities.

Mio padre ha condiviso con me un suo ricordo del nonno che credo rappresenti davvero la sua personalità speciale.

All'inizio degli anni '30, prima di sposarsi e di iniziare a lavorare sui tram, il nonno aprì un piccolo negozio di alimentari in South Jamaica, un quartiere residenziale nel distretto di Queens, a New York, tra Sutphin Blvd e Rockaway Blvd. Per chi non dovesse conoscere bene New York City, Jamaica era—ed è tuttora—un quartiere piuttosto povero, in cui abitano molte famiglie bisognose. Nonno conosceva bene la zona e volle cogliere l'occasione per aprire un'attività in proprio.

Da quel momento, divenne rapidamente noto in tutto il quartiere, grazie al suo carattere estroverso e al suo modo gentile di preoccuparsi sinceramente delle persone che risiedevano lì. I bambini della zona amavano passare dal negozio, perché sapevano che il nonno avrebbe regalato loro con gioia qualche caramella o dolcetto da gustare. Più passava il tempo, più la sua generosità aumentava.

Quando arrivava qualcuno che non poteva pagare l'importo totale, il nonno lasciava loro ciò che desideravano accettando la somma che potevano permettersi, tanto che arrivò ad un punto in cui regalava più di quanto effettivamente vendesse. Sicuramente molto generoso da parte sua, ma terribile per il profitto del negozio.

Magari non era tagliato per essere un grande imprenditore, ma aveva le sue buone ragioni. Non riusciva a non empatizzare con queste persone, si metteva nei loro panni perché un tempo anche lui aveva vissuto in tali condizioni. Quando vieni dal nulla non puoi dimenticare come ci si senta, e il nonno non lo fece mai. In qualunque momento della vita si trovasse, dava tutto quello che poteva, ogni volta che poteva.

Nonno and Nonna with their son Francesco; Nonno's paesano Nico Pascaluce and brother-in-law Dominic

Dandelions
denti di leone

You will need:
1 bunch of dandelions
garlic (4–6 cloves; sliced or chopped)
extra virgin olive oil (4–6 second pour)
salt to taste
water
¼ teaspoon of salt for water

Required pots:
1 large pot, 1 frying pan

Nonno's tip:
I loved picking dandelions along my daily walks for this recipe! Dandelions can be bitter, so the rule is that larger ones are good for soup, while smaller ones are more tender and less bitter, great for this recipe.

Bring a large pot of water to boil.

Wash and cut ¼–½ inch off the bottom of the greens.

Add salt just before adding greens to the pot.

Let boil for 3–5 minutes, remove and drain.

In a large frying pan, heat oil then add garlic and let brown.

Add the greens (it will splatter so be prepared!)

Zeza

The "Zeza di Bellizzi" is a show that dates back to the 1600s and has folk song and dance. The show has Neapolitan origins, the same area where Nonno is from in Italy, and was originally created to entertain the nobles. It quickly became a faithful regional tradition that went on to be performed all throughout theaters and Carnivals in Italy.

Southern Italian immigrants brought the performance to the USA and carried it on in local communities, preserving the costumes and casting, but making changes to the dialogue. The story is pretty simple and has two main characters called Zeza (Lucrezia) and Pulcinella. However, when the show was created back in the 1600s, women were not permitted to perform, so male actors played all the female parts. This is a feature that stayed with the "Zeza di Bellizzi" to this day.

With Nonno being from that part of the world, he thoroughly enjoyed the "Zeza" and often performed in it. It's a lively show and at the end, there is a large dance called the "Quadriglia" where the whole ensemble sings and dances together. When this is done on the streets or Carnivals, the audience joins in the dance as well.

Nonno never missed the opportunity to be a part of something that had to do with his heritage. He also never missed the opportunity to laugh and have fun. As wise as he was and as serious as he could be, he could flip that coin and be the funniest person in the room. I'll always admire him for that.

Espressione di un'antica tradizione popolare di origini napoletane, ovvero della provincia italiana da cui proviene il nonno, la "Zeza di Bellizzi" è uno spettacolo che risale al 1600, caratterizzato da canti e danze popolari e originariamente creato per intrattenere la nobiltà. Divenuta in poco tempo un'importante manifestazione di cultura, amore, passione e tradizione regionale, è rappresentata tutt'oggi in tutti i teatri e carnevali d'Italia.

Gli immigrati provenienti dall'Italia meridionale portarono con sé lo spettacolo negli Stati Uniti, e continuarono a rappresentarlo nelle comunità locali, preservando costumi e casting ma apportando alcune modifiche ai dialoghi. La trama, i cui due personaggi principali sono chiamati Zeza (Lucrezia) e Pulcinella, è piuttosto semplice. Tuttavia, nel lontano 1600, ai tempi in cui lo spettacolo fu creato, alle donne non era permesso esibirsi, quindi erano gli attori maschi che interpretavano tutti i ruoli femminili; tale peculiarità è rimasta inalterata fino ad oggi.

Avendo avuto origini proprio nelle terre del nonno, la "Zeza di Bellizzi" era per lui di grande importanza e vi si esibiva spesso. È uno spettacolo molto movimentato, che si conclude con un grande ballo chiamato la "Quadriglia", dove l'intero complesso musicale canta e balla assieme. Quando la manifestazione si svolge per le strade o durante i carnevali, il pubblico si unisce alla danza.

Nonno Angelo non si lasciava mai scappare l'opportunità di partecipare a qualunque evento che avesse a che fare con il suo patrimonio culturale, così come non perdeva mai l'occasione di ridere e divertirsi. Era un uomo saggio e alle volte serio, ma aveva la capacità di trasformarsi in un secondo e diventare la persona più divertente del mondo. Avrà sempre la mia ammirazione, per questo oltre che per mille altri motivi.

the clown

Elmer

Elmer & Massone

Mamma clown daughter Priest priest

Massone Elmer Angelo Ascar

Happy Birthday Dear Angelo
1903 Zeza-zeza-play 1993

Anthony Stringile wrote this

Play from zeza-zeza record

and four paesano (they grew
up together) Mariglianella Napoli
                        Italy
Elmer Esposito = as a clown
ascar   "   = as a priest
Massimo Di Monde - as a mother
Angelo Tovino as Massimo daughter
          ready to get married.

This must been a great play for
        Hallowin (and good time)

Mushrooms with lemon and butter
funghi con limone e burro

You will need:
1 large container of button mushrooms (sliced to preference)
½ stick of butter
1–2 lemons
pinch of salt

Required pots:
1 saucepan

Nonno's tip:
Put a note in your serving dish to help remind yourself to add the lemon before serving!

In a saucepan, melt the butter over medium heat and add the mushrooms, stirring to coat them.

Add salt and cook for 5 minutes.

Cover and let cook for 10–15 minutes.

The mushrooms should've reduced ½–¼ in size and when they are tender remove from heat and let stand.

When ready to serve, heat through and add lemon.

Braciole
braciole

You will need:
**Braciole meat from any
  Italian butcher**
**garlic (1–2 sliced; per piece
  of meat)**
1 tablespoon pine nuts
1 tablespoon raisins
2 tablespoons grating cheese
2 tablespoons parsley
**extra virgin olive oil
  (2 second pour)**
pinch of salt
twine to tie

Nonno's tip:
Cook these in Sunday gravy or eat
separately.

On a clean surface, lay the meat
down flat.

Spread garlic, parsley, pine nuts,
raisins, grating cheese, salt and
drizzle of EVOO across meat.

Roll up meat vertically and
tie with twine.*

You can brown these by
themselves or with the neck bone.

---

* I never saw my grandparents
with butchers twine. They always
used the twine that tied up the box
from the Italian bakery.

nonno's moderation

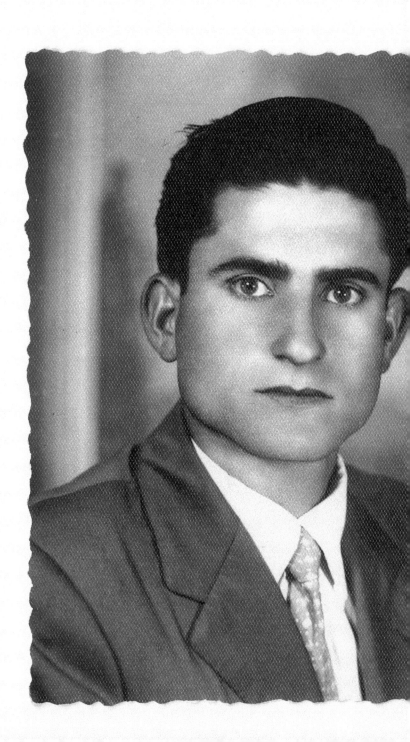

If there is one thing I admire most about my Nonno, it was his belief that life was lived best in moderation. He always had this beautiful way of balance and never let himself get out of control with anything. It's as if he never let something get the best of him, and I didn't realize until I've gotten a little older just how hard that is for most people.

He would make these wonderful meals but he wouldn't overeat and stuff himself into a food coma. Imagine making a couple dozen tasty meatballs only to eat two or so a week so you could truly savor them when you had them—that's what Nonno did regularly! He'd freeze them and every week have a couple until he ran out and then he'd make another batch.

Similar to eating, Nonno also didn't over-drink. He would certainly enjoy a glass of homemade red wine but never sit back and drink the whole bottle. I don't think anyone can say they ever saw him drunk on any occasion. He knew how much was just enough for him and didn't feel the need to go further than that.

Nonno also took daily walks, ensuring his body and mind got the movement and stimulation they required. Like I've already mentioned, Nonno didn't have a driver's license so walking was a huge part of his life, but the importance of physical exercise was always relevant to him. He created his own workout equipment using materials he found around the house. On the other side of that, Nonno would take naps and get a good night's sleep regularly. He valued rest and knew he wouldn't be up to par by his own standards if he was operating off minimal sleep.

One thing that was really popular back then was soaking your feet at the end of the day and that stayed with Nonno. He never failed to soak his feet every single night of his life. I have many memories of filling up the basin with water for his nightly soak as do my sisters and father. It was a part of his routine, a part of his schedule, and after walking several miles a day it was well deserved. He taught us that not only does soaking your feet feel nice but it also has several healing qualities, as it is detoxing for your body.

Se devo scegliere una sola qualità della personalità del nonno, tra le tante che ammiro, è la sua temperanza in ogni aspetto della vita e la convinzione che tale caratteristica possa farti vivere al meglio. Ha sempre avuto questo innato e ammirevole senso di equilibrio: aveva la capacità di rimanere composto, non si faceva mai sopraffare dalle emozioni o dalle situazioni, e mi resi conto solo avanti con gli anni di quanto ciò sia difficile per la maggior parte delle persone.

Preparava ogni giorno pasti squisiti, ma non avrebbe mai mangiato così tanto da sentirsi male Ad esempio, preparava una ventina di deliziose polpette e ne mangiava solamente un paio a settimana, in modo da potersele davvero gustare. E così faceva regolarmente con diverse pietanze! Cucinava varie porzioni, congelava quelle in eccesso e le consumava a poco a poco finché non finivano, per poi prepararne altre porzioni per le settimane a seguire, e così via.

Come con il cibo, nonno Angelo non esagerava mai neanche con l'alcool. Sapeva certamente godersi ogni tanto un bicchiere di vino rosso della casa, ma non gli sarebbe mai passata per la testa l'idea di bersi l'intera bottiglia. Non credo che nessuno l'abbia mai visto ubriaco in nessuna occasione. Sapeva semplicemente riconoscere il suo limite e non sentiva il bisogno di andare oltre.

Il nonno, inoltre, usciva a passeggiare quotidianamente, assicurandosi che sia il corpo che la mente ricevessero il movimento e gli stimoli di cui avevano bisogno ogni giorno. Come ho accennato precedentemente, non aveva la patente, quindi il camminare occupava per forza di cose una parte molto importante della sua vita. A prescindere dalla necessità di spostarsi, l'esercizio fisico è sempre stato per lui di fondamentale importanza. Si costruiva da solo l'attrezzatura per allenarsi, utilizzando materiali che trovava in giro per casa. Amava muoversi, ma amava anche i suoi preziosi sonnellini pomeridiani e aveva una routine di sonno notturno molto regolare. Sapeva apprezzare quindi anche il riposo, consapevole del fatto che la sua produttività durante la giornata era strettamente legata alla qualità delle sue ore di sonno.

Un'attività molto comune allora era mettere a mollo i piedi a fine giornata, cosa che il nonno fece per l'appunto ogni singola sera della sua vita. Sia io che mio papà e le mie sorelle abbiamo molti ricordi di noi che a turno riempiamo la bacinella d'acqua per l'ammollo serale; faceva semplicemente parte della sua routine e del suo programma quotidiano. D'altronde, dopo aver camminato svariati chilometri in una sola giornata, era un trattamento più che meritato! Ecco un'altra preziosa conoscenza che ci ha trasmesso: immergere i piedi in acqua non solo è piacevole, ma ha anche molteplici qualità curative in quanto è considerata un'attività disintossicante per il corpo.

Nonno's life of moderation and Mediterranean diet included medicinal herbs and vitamins like Rose Hips. Rose Hips are found just below the rose petals and are beneficial for their vitamin C and their ability to combat different types of arthritis. He had them every morning along with his fresh squeezed orange juice and his È Mort (see recipe at page 23) without fail.

Like most old school men, Nonno wasn't a big fan of the doctors but he took care of his health in a more holistic way. Every three or four months he would get a vitamin B-12 shot to help maintain a healthy immune system and energy level. He would also visit a chiropractor once a week until he was 80-something years old. For Nonno, this is what worked best.

Nonno's inner awareness and self-control was so powerful, it's no question to me that it contributed to his long and healthy life. He used every resource he could to better himself and showed us that if you love yourself then you should respect yourself.

La vita quotidiana del nonno, caratterizzata da temperanza e dieta mediterranea, includeva l'utilizzo di erbe medicinali e di vitamine come i cinorrodi: questi ultimi sono i falsi frutti delle rose ad alto contenuto di vitamina C e dalle diverse proprietà benefiche, come ad esempio la capacità di combattere diversi tipi di artrite. Li prendeva ogni singola mattina insieme al suo succo d'arancia e l'È Mort (vedi ricetta a pagina 23).

Come la maggior parte degli uomini di una volta, nonno non amava molto i medici e la medicina tradizionale, preferiva prendersi cura della sua salute con un approccio maggiormente olistico. Puntualmente ogni tre o quattro mesi riceveva un'iniezione di vitamina B-12, la cui funzione è mantenere sano il sistema immunitario e un buon livello di energia. Inoltre, una volta alla settimana si recava da un chiropratico, fino al raggiungimento degli 80 anni.

La sua consapevolezza interiore e la capacità di autocontrollo erano così forti, che per me non c'è dubbio che abbiano avuto una grande influenza positiva nel suo trascorrere una vita lunga e sana. Lo sviluppo personale era per lui una priorità, utilizzava ogni risorsa in suo potere per migliorarsi continuamente, mostrandoci quanto è importante amare e di conseguenza rispettare sé stessi.

Nonno's paesano Pascaluce and his family

Eggplant
melanzane

You will need:
tomato sauce (home made)
1 eggplant
dredging flour
¼ teaspoon salt
1 egg (beaten)
olive oil for frying
bread crumbs (1–2 cups)
grating cheese (2 cups)
½ cup fresh parsley and basil
  (optional)
a pinch of salt for finished batch

This is an individual serving but simply multiply the recipe to accommodate your needs.

Required pots:
1 frying pan, 1 ovenproof or Pyrex dish

Nonno's tip:
Let these stay warm in the oven until ready to be served.

In a separate bowl, mix bread crumbs, grating cheese, salt, parsley, and basil.

Slice eggplant into ⅛–¼ inch pieces.

Coat eggplant in flour, then egg, then the breadcrumbs. Place on a plate while you prepare the rest.

In a frying pan, add enough olive oil to cover the bottom of the pan to a medium-high heat.

Lay eggplants into pan (facing away from you) as oil is hot. Generally a pan can hold 6–8 pieces.

After a few minutes, check one until it's coming brown and then flip with fork or tongs.

When the other side is cooking, place a brown bag over a plate to drain.

Add a pinch of salt while hot.

Now the eggplant is finished and ready to eat. If you'd like to add more flavor, this is a great next step.

Heat oven to 200–250°.

Add tomato sauce to bottom of ovenproof dish and place 3–4 pieces of eggplant on top of it.

Layer with more tomato sauce and a dusting of grating cheese. Repeat for 3 layers max.

Keep warm until ready to serve.

Canned tuna with appetizer

tonno in scatola con caponata
di melanzane

You will need:
1 can of tuna
1 can of eggplant appetizer

Nonno's tip:
Canned eggplant appetizer is
extremely versatile for many
different recipes!

Drain tuna.

Mix tuna and eggplant appetizer in
a bowl together.

Mix and serve, with crusty bread
or eat as is.

**Canned tuna with red cabbage
and lemon**
tonno in scatola con cavolo rosso
e limone

You will need:
¼ **head of red cabbage
   (sliced thin)**
1 **can of tuna**
1 **lemon**
**extra virgin olive oil
   (2–3 second pour)**
2–3 **tablespoons of capers
   (optional)**
pinch of salt

Nonno's tip:
Always keep some tuna cans in
your pantry—they come in handy.

In a bowl, add cabbage, lemon
juice, salt, EVOO and mix.

Add tuna and mix again lightly.

Serve as a sandwich, with crackers
or as is!

67   A timeline of love, a look at Nonno and Nonna through their lives together. Amore forever.

nonna Rose

There are some kinds of love you know you can only explain as magical. That was what my Nonno and Nonna had. I remember the way they looked at each other; it was enough to melt the coldest heart. They loved each other in a way only soul mates could.

Nonna Rose was born in New York City on April 1, 1911. Her family was from Mariglianella, in the province of Napoli, which is the same town Nonno's family was from. You could say their fate to find each other was arranged in the stars. In any case, it was anything but coincidence.

While Nonno was an amazing cook, Nonna Rose ran the kitchen while she was alive. In my mind, every meal she made could've been served to royalty—especially her eggplant parmigiana! That was the first meal she taught me how to cook and it's still one of my favorites. She sincerely enjoyed feeding her family and seeing their elation after a big bite. Like a true rose, every room was better with Nonna Rose in it.

Among my favorite memories of all time are Nonna Rose's birthdays. My Nonno would make her a cake made out of cardboard with real whipped cream frosting because she was born on April Fools Day. He would top the cake with candles and bring it out to her as we all sang Happy Birthday, and she'd play along with the whole thing. Every time she went to slice the cake, she would act surprised that it was cardboard. I mean, Nonno did this every year and every year she'd have this big surprised reaction that was totally hilarious for the family to watch. Then, all the kids would eat the whipped cream and toppings while the adults drank wine and spent the rest of the day together.

Unfortunately, Nonna Rose had some physical ailments that made her life a bit more difficult. She had severe asthma and on top of that she'd taken a bad fall where she ended up breaking her hip and lived out the rest of her life wheelchair-bound. But, Nonna Rose never showed any type of stress or dismay.

My father told me one of his strongest memories of Nonna Rose, his mother, was that despite all of her physical pain, she never complained once. In fact, she did just the opposite. She was playful and adoring. She was a precious woman who made everyone around her feel loved.

Nonna Rose passed away December 20, 1985. Nonno's devotion to her never faded and he never had interest in anyone else. He never gave up on life but he gave up on love the day she died. But just like Nonna Rose would stay positive, so

Ci sono storie d'amore che non si possono spiegare. Semplicemente magiche, come quella dei miei nonni. Ricordo ancora il modo in cui si guardavano, avrebbe sciolto anche il cuore più freddo… si amavano come solamente due anime gemelle avrebbero potuto fare.

Nonna Rose nacque a New York il 1° aprile del 1911. La sua famiglia era originaria di Mariglianella, in provincia di Napoli, lo stesso borgo da cui proveniva la famiglia del nonno. Che fossero destinati a trovarsi era scritto nelle stelle, e fu tutt'altro che una coincidenza.

Il nonno era un cuoco straordinario, ma la vera capa della cucina, finché rimase in vita, era nonna Rose. Da quel che mi ricordo, ogni pasto da lei preparato poteva essere servito alla famiglia reale, specialmente la sua parmigiana di melanzane! Fu il primo piatto che mi insegnò a cucinare e rimane tutt'ora uno dei miei preferiti. Far da mangiare alla famiglia e vedere la gioia sul loro viso dopo il primo boccone le riempiva il cuore. Come una vera e bellissima rosa, ogni stanza in cui appariva nonna Rose prendeva improvvisamente luce e colore.

Tra i miei ricordi preferiti di sempre ci sono i compleanni della nonna Rose, quando per la speciale occasione il nonno le preparava una finta torta di cartone coperta di una vera glassa di panna montata… pesce d'aprile!

Riempiva la torta di candeline e gliela portava mentre tutti, lei compresa, cantavamo la canzoncina di buon compleanno. Al momento del taglio della torta, ogni anno si mostrava sorpresa nello scoprire che fosse di cartone. Eppure il nonno proponeva lo stesso scherzo ogni anno, e lei pur di stare al gioco faceva finta di dimenticarsene; ogni volta era uno spettacolo esilarante per tutta la famiglia! La festa proseguiva poi con tutti i più piccoli che giustamente si mangiavano la panna montata, mentre gli adulti condividevano bicchieri di vino e chiacchiere per il resto della giornata.

Purtroppo, la nonna durante il corso della sua vita ebbe alcuni disturbi fisici che le resero la vita un po' complicata. Aveva un grave asma e, come se non bastasse, subì una brutta caduta che portò alla rottura dell'anca, e da quel momento fu costretta a vivere il resto della sua vita sulla sedia a rotelle. Forte com'era, tuttavia, non si mostrava mai in alcun modo stressata o amareggiata dai suoi problemi fisici.

Mio padre era solito raccontarmi di come la nonna Rose, ovvero sua madre, non si lamentasse mai, nonostante il dolore fisico che sopportava ogni giorno. Piuttosto, il suo atteggiamento era all'esatto opposto: era gioiosa, scherzosa, spensierata. Era una donna davvero speciale, nata con il prezioso dono di far sentire amati tutti coloro che la circondavano.

would my Nonno. He always said that in his heart he knew that the day he left this world, she would be there waiting for him, and that was all that mattered. Nonno's favorite flowers were roses and he grew them in his yard. He would graft new bushes and give them to friends and family in Nonna Rose's honor. Roses will always have a special place in my family's gardens.

Nonna Rose ci lasciò il 20 dicembre del 1985. L'amore e la devozione di nonno nei suoi confronti fecero sì che lui mai e poi mai si interessasse ad un'altra donna. Non rinunciò mai alla sua vita, ma il giorno in cui dovettero separarsi rinunciò all'amore. Rimase nonostante ciò molto positivo, come la nonna avrebbe fatto al posto suo. Diceva sempre che nel suo cuore sapeva che il giorno in cui sarebbe toccato a lui lasciare questo mondo, lei sarebbe stata lì ad aspettarlo, e questo era tutto ciò che contava.

I fiori preferiti del nonno sono le rose; da quel momento iniziò a coltivarle in giardino. Faceva innesti di nuove piantine e le donava ad amici e parenti in onore della nonna. Le rose avranno sempre un posto speciale nei giardini della mia famiglia.

Check out Nonno's Courtyard and his online community, share your own Meals and Memories there at www.mealsandmemorieswithnonno.com

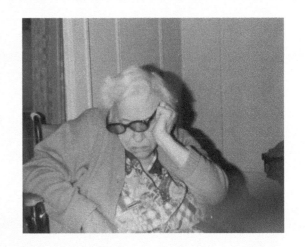

Nonna Rose and I; Nonno's daughter-in-law Barbara

Zucchini flowers "pizzette"
pizzette di fiori di zucca

You will need:
12 or more zucchini flowers
1 cup flour
½–¾ cup of water
extra virgin olive oil
pinch of salt

Required pots:
1 frying pan

Nonno's tip:
First thing, make sure there is not a bee inside your zucchini flower!

Zucchini flowers can be hard to come by, you have to look for them. If you want to grow a zucchini plant or know someone who has one, that's the best way to have flowers. You need the flower that has a stem or the flower at the end of the fruit (just don't pick the flower until the fruit is 2–3 inches long).

After checking for bees, rinse flowers and pat dry.

Mix flour in a bowl, then slowly add water, about ¼ cup at a time (the consistency should be like loose pancake batter).

In a separate pan, add EVOO and heat.

Add batter to pan so you have a pancake, about 3 inches.

Place 1 or 2 of the zucchini flowers in the center, flip and cook until golden brown.

Place on a brown paper bag to drain.

Add salt just before serving.

You can also stuff these with chopped tomato, garlic, cheese or any filling you'd like, or add to pasta with garlic and oil.

Marinated zucchini
with peppermint
zucchine marinate
con menta piperita

You will need:
2 whole zucchini
garlic (6 cloves; sliced)
oregano
fresh peppermint
vinegar
extra virgin olive oil
   (a few 2–4 second pours)

Nonno's tip:
Go light on the oregano and
vinegar in this recipe, as they are
both powerful ingredients, but use
the peppermint on every layer!

Slice zucchini about the width of
a quarter.

In a frying pan, add EVOO and
sliced zucchini.

Once tender, remove and place on
brown paper bag. Keep the EVOO
as you will need it for the rest of
the zucchini slices.

In a glass bowl or old jar, put down
a layer of zucchini, then garlic,
sprinkle of oregano, a dash of
vinegar, 2–3 peppermint leaves and
repeat multiple times.

75   Nonno's sister Rachlele and brother-in-law Vincenzo with their daughter Rafaelina

plants and nature

Nonno was a very resourceful man and it wasn't because he didn't have money. He grew up on a farm in Italy and loved the earth very much. From the moment he was able to walk, he started helping his mother with her herbs and helping his dad in the fields. Nonno's father actually passed away in the fields moving big stones while they were farming and Nonno was only a young boy. For that time and that profession, it was just a way of life.

Growing up working with the land, Nonno knew the value of it. He would plant his peach pits from lunch alongside the Belt Parkway until they eventually started growing into peach trees. A simple seed was capable of providing so much if taken care of and Nonno honored that.

Nonno and Nonna Rose were completely in tune with nature and animals. They knew they were a part of this bigger world and what mattered most was how you treat all living things. Material items were never something they really cared about so long as they had a few good kitchen pots and a roof over their heads.

I remember they used to hand feed the squirrels peanuts in the backyard every day. They named each one of them after deceased family members and would carry on conversations like "Did you see Frankie today?" or "Maria looks like she hasn't eaten much." They had a couple dozen squirrels at one point and could tell the difference between each one.

The squirrels would sometimes get anxious for their food and would come up to the back door and scratch on it. You'd hear Nonna Rose say, "Oh Rachele wants to see Angelo!" and my Nonno would come over with a bag of peanuts ready to feed it. It was one of their daily activities, along with feeding the birds, and being a part of the world around them.

Possiamo definire il nonno come un uomo dalle mille risorse, e non perché non fosse abbastanza abbiente. Cresciuto in una tipica fattoria del sud Italia, amava la terra e la natura con tutto il cuore. Non appena fu in grado di camminare, iniziò ad aiutare la madre con la cura delle erbe aromatiche e a dare una mano al padre nei campi. Purtroppo, suo padre morì proprio lavorando nei campi spostando dei grossi massi, quando il nonno era solo un ragazzino. Per quell'epoca e quella professione, si trattava semplicemente di un comune incidente relazionato con lo stile di vita.

Essendo cresciuto lavorando la terra, il nonno ne conosceva bene il valore e i segreti. Conservava i noccioli delle pesche del pranzo e li piantava lungo la Belt Parkway, ed ecco che dopo un po' iniziavano a spuntare gli alberi di pesco. Se era il nonno a prendersene cura, un semplice seme avrebbe prodotto tantissimi frutti.

Nonno Angelo e Nonna Rose vivevano in totale sintonia con la natura e gli animali attorno a loro. Sapevano di essere solo una piccola parte di un mondo molto più vasto, e che ciò che contava davvero era il modo in cui venivano trattati tutti gli altri esseri viventi. Non si preoccupavano mai troppo di possedere oggetti materiali, a loro bastavano alcune buone pentole da cucina e un tetto sopra la testa.

Ricordo che, ogni giorno, davano da mangiare delle noccioline agli scoiattoli che spuntavano nel cortile dietro casa. Avevano assegnato ad ognuno di loro il nome di un parente deceduto e, durante le conversazioni quotidiane, si riferivano a loro come dei veri e propri membri della famiglia, ad esempio: "Hai visto Frankie oggi?" oppure: "Mi sa che Maria oggi non ha mangiato un granché" Ad un certo punto avevano addirittura assegnato un nome ad una ventina di scoiattoli e riuscivano incredibilmente a distinguerli l'uno dall'altro.

Gli scoiattoli a volte, ansiosi di ricevere la loro porzione di cibo, si avvicinavano alla porta sul retro e iniziavano a graffiarla. A quel punto nonna Rose esclamava: "Oh, Angelo, Leonardo ti sta chiamando!" e mio nonno arrivava con un sacchetto di noccioline pronto per dargli da mangiare. Era una delle loro tante attività quotidiane, come nutrire gli uccellini ed essere parte integrante del mondo che li circondava.

Since Nonno never got a driver's license, he walked everywhere or had someone drive him. But he walked most of the time and we used to walk to the Belmont Race Track along the Long Island Railroad Tracks. That's easily about 5–6 miles one way.

After the races, he would take me to the Cross Island Parkway where we would stop and pick dandelions and mushrooms to cook with later. No matter if he won or lost at the racetrack, we were going to eat well. When I asked why he always chose to pick things from the side of the highway he said it was because he didn't have to worry about people walking their dogs there—and where there are no dogs there is no dog poop. Nonno instinctively knew things that most people require explanations for.

Nonno was eating watercress way before it was a popular menu item in the United States. When he was reassigned to the Parks Department in the 1940s, he met an Asian family on one of his walks that was harvesting watercress along the natural springs and creeks.

From them, he learned how to sow the seed himself and started growing it as well to feed

Siccome il nonno non prese mai la patente, era solito spostarsi a piedi ovunque, oppure si faceva portare in macchina da qualcuno. La maggior parte delle volte decideva comunque di camminare; per esempio, andavamo sempre a piedi al Belmont Park lungo la Long Island Railroad, una decina di km solo andata.

Dopo aver assistito alle corse dei cavalli, mi portava sempre alla Cross Island Parkway, dove ci fermavamo a raccogliere denti di leone e funghi che avremmo poi utilizzato per cucinare.

Che i suoi cavalli vincessero o perdessero poco importava, l'importante era mangiare bene dopo e ovviamente i pasti non deludevano mai! Alla mia domanda sul perché scegliesse di raccogliere sempre questi prodotti della natura a lato dell'autostrada, rispose che così non avrebbe dovuto preoccuparsi delle persone che portavano i cani a passeggiare nella zona, perché dove non ci sono cani non ci sono neanche i loro escrementi. Il suo istinto gli suggeriva sempre sagge risposte alle domande alle quali la maggior parte delle persone non saprebbe rispondere.

Nonno Angelo mangiava il crescione molto prima che diventasse una voce di menu molto popolare negli Stati Uniti. Quando fu assegnato nuovamente al Dipartimento dei Parchi Urbani negli anni '40, durante una delle sue passeggiate incontrò una famiglia asiatica che raccoglieva il crescione lungo le sorgenti naturali e i torrenti. Fu un incontro fortunato, perché proprio da loro imparò a seminarlo e coltivarlo, per poterlo cucinare per la famiglia. Sicuramente non erano molti gli italiani che consumavano crescione negli anni '40! Amava avere sempre nuovi stimoli del genere, poiché gli tenevano la mente e il corpo occupati allo stesso tempo.

La passione del nonno per i suoi orti di verdure si poteva definire molto meticolosa. Studiava con attenzione le varie fasi lunari per sapere esattamente quali verdure piantare e in quali giorni. Ad esempio, sapeva che le piante piccole dovevano essere piantate con la luna piena,

his family. There were definitely not many Italians eating watercress in the 1940s! He always loved having new stimuli like this, since they kept his mind and body busy.

Nonno's passion for his vegetable gardens was precise. He studied the phases of the moon in order to know which vegetables to plant on what days. For instance, he knew it was better to plant small plants on a full moon because the moon would give it extra sunlight. If you ever go out on a full moon, in fact, you'll notice you have a shadow.

He inspired so many of us throughout our lives to connect with the earth like he did. Sure, maybe we can't all have expansive vegetable gardens like Nonno, but the act of planting a seed and helping it grow into something bigger can be done just about anywhere.

No matter the size, you can start small, but just start.

perché l'effetto della luna avrebbe garantito loro maggior luce solare. Se ti capita di uscire in strada con la luna piena, noterai infatti di avere un'ombra.

Con il suo stile di vita e il suo lavoro nei campi, ha ispirato tanti di noi della famiglia ad entrare in connessione con la natura nello stesso modo in cui

lo faceva lui. Certo, non tutti forse possiamo avere orti così ricchi di verdure come quelli del nonno, ma anche solo il semplice atto di piantare un seme, prendersene cura e aiutarlo a maturare può essere fatto praticamente ovunque. Non importano le dimensioni, se vuoi iniziare, fallo in piccolo.

String beans & sausage
with potatoes
fagiolini e salsiccia con patate

You will need:
Italian sausage (4–6 links)
garlic (6–8 cloves)
½ onion
2 potatoes (small–medium size)
**1–1½ pounds of fresh string
beans**
8–12 plum tomatoes in season
basil (6–10 leaves)
½ teaspoon of salt
**extra virgin olive oil
(3–4 second pour)**
grating cheese

This recipe calls for the potatoes
and string beans to be cooked
beforehand. Save the water from
these, as you will need to use it in
the recipe.

Required pots:
1 small roasting pan with lid,
1 large pot

Nonno's tip:
Save time and dice the tomatoes and
other vegetables while the potatoes
and string beans are cooking.

How do you know when it's
done? You want it to be the perfect
consistency. If it's too loose, add
some liquid from the potatoes.
If it's too thick, add some liquid
from the string beans.

Sausage:
Heat oven to 450°

Add sausage to the small roasting
pan and fill with water until halfway.

Cover the pan and cook for 20–30
minutes.

The rest:
Slice garlic and onion and set aside.

Cut cooked potatoes into quarters
and set aside.

Cut string beans into 3 inch pieces
and set aside.

Dice tomatoes and set aside.

In the large pot, heat the EVOO
and add the onion and garlic and
sauté for 3–5 minutes then add salt.

When the onion and garlic are
almost brown, add the tomatoes
and ½ of your basil leaves.
Sauté for 5–10 minutes until the
tomatoes begin to soften.

Add potatoes, string beans and
some of the string bean water and
bring to a boil. Let simmer for
5–10 minutes covered.

Taste and see if you can pick up
all the flavors, especially the string
beans. Add some of the potato
water to thicken up the mixture.

When sausage is cooked, cut each
one into 3 pieces and add it to the
mixture. You can add some of
the liquid from the sausage too if
you'd like. Stir and enjoy!

82   Nonno's niece Rafaelina on her wedding day

Meatballs
polpette

At any Italian family dinner, there is a good chance you'll hear meatball recipes flying in every direction. This is the Iovine family recipe.

Se ti capiterà di essere invitato ad una cena di famiglia in Italia, probabilmente sentirai ogni persona presente proporre la propria versione di ricetta di polpette di carne. Questa è la ricetta della famiglia Iovine.

You will need:
1 lb of chop meat (not lean)
garlic (6–8 cloves, chopped)
1 onion (chopped)
½ bunch of fresh parsley
grating cheese (½ cup)
½–1 loaf of stale Italian bread (<u>no bread crumbs!</u>)
1–2 eggs
water (enough for the bread to soak in)
pine nuts and raisins (optional; ⅛ cup of each)

Required pots:
1 frying pan or baking sheet

Nonno's tip:
What you're looking for is 50/50 or 60/40 of chopped meat to bread ratio in this recipe, depending how you like your texture.

Take ½ loaf of stale bread and soak in water until mushy then drain and squeeze.

In a separate bowl, add soaked bread and chopped meat (about 50/50), then add the rest of the ingredients except the eggs.

Using your hands, give it a quick mix, then add egg by beating yolk with finger in the mixture.

Mix should be able to bind together and hold. If it's not, add additional egg.

Form mixture into balls and prepare to fry or bake.

Fry at medium heat until brown or bake at 350° for 30–45 minutes depending on your oven.

sunday dinner

It's no secret that Italian families generally have Sunday dinner together. Of course when we say dinner, what we mean is sometime around 1–2 pm. In Nonno and Nonna's house, everyone looked forward to Sunday because not only were we going to eat delectable food, but also we were going to spend time with each other. It was always busy with my aunts, uncles, cousins and friends coming and going throughout the day.

Every Sunday dinner at Nonno's was a seven course meal. That's not including the antipasto that would be put out while they finished preparing the

Le famiglie italiane, com'è ben noto, si riuniscono per cenare insieme ogni domenica. Ciò che noi chiamiamo cena è in realtà un pranzo sul tardi, intorno alle 14:00. A casa dei nonni, la famiglia non vedeva l'ora che arrivasse quell'appuntamento settimanale; sapevamo che avremmo mangiato come dei re e, soprattutto, che avremmo trascorso del tempo prezioso tutti insieme.

Ogni "cena" della domenica da nonno comprendeva un pasto composto da sette portate, tra le quali non era neanche incluso l'antipasto, che portavano fuori mentre finivano di preparare le altre

rest of the food. My mouth still salivates as I recall the aroma of walking into their house on these days. A menu usually consisted of something like:

Salad
Chicken
Pasta
Meat
Eggplant
Fruit
Dessert

Nonno would start preparing early on Sunday morning, usually before the sun would rise. As you'll notice troughout the book, many of the recipes—particularly the Sunday gravy—have to cook for quite a while on a low heat. However, Sunday mornings were a busy time for Nonno and he'd often have to run out for an errand or Sunday Mass.

So, he'd keep the stove on a low simmer when he had to leave the house. My family and I would take him on his errands because remember Nonno didn't drive and when he was out of ear shot we'd say to each other "I wonder if the house is on fire yet." Nobody questioned him or asked if he was worried about a fire because we knew he wasn't. We'd always expect to get back to the gravy burnt or the house completely up in flames but it never was.

Now I am not encouraging you to leave the stove on when you leave the house. In fact, I recommend that you don't ever do that. Listen, I don't know how he did it—it's just part of Nonno's magic. He was amazingly confident in everything, that he just knew how to pull it off.

pietanze. Ho ancora l'acquolina in bocca al pensiero del profumino che si sentiva entrando in casa quelle domeniche. Il menù, solitamente, consisteva in:

Insalata
Pollo
Pasta
Carne
Melanzane
Frutta
Dolce

Nonno Angelo iniziava la grande preparazione al mattino presto, prima ancora che il sole sorgesse. Come noterai leggendo questo libro, molte delle ricette descritte—tra queste in particolare il sugo della domenica—necessitano di una cottura lunga e a fuoco lento. La domenica mattina, tuttavia, il nonno aveva sempre un gran daffare, spesso doveva correre fuori per commissioni dell'ultimo momento oppure per assistere alla messa.

Molto spesso lasciava quindi il fuoco acceso con la fiamma bassa, mentre io ed altri membri della famiglia lo portavamo a fare le sue commissioni, sempre per il fatto che non aveva la patente. Facendo in modo che il nonno non sentisse, ci dicevamo sempre: "chissà se la casa sarà ancora intera oppure in fiamme". Non gli chiedevamo mai se fosse preoccupato per un possibile incendio, perché sapevamo che non lo era. E nonostante noi una leggera paura di tornare e trovare la casa bruciata ce l'avessimo davvero, per fortuna non è mai stato questo il caso.

Con questo non ti sto incoraggiando a lasciare senza problemi i fornelli accesi quando esci di casa, anzi, ti consiglio vivamente di non farlo mai. Non so proprio come facesse, faceva anche questo parte delle sue doti straordinarie. Grazie alla sua fermissima fiducia nelle proprie capacità, alla fine in qualche modo se la cavava sempre in ogni situazione.

Share Meals and Memories of your own and join Nonno's online community on our website! www.mealsandmemorieswithnonno.com

Sunday gravy with meat
ragù napoletano

You will need:
2 cans (32 oz) of whole or
    crushed tomatoes with basil
    (San Marzano, if possible)
1 can tomato paste
garlic (6–8 cloves, chopped)
½ onion (chopped)
extra virgin olive oil
    (6–8 second pour)
¼ teaspoon salt
⅜ cup of grating cheese
fresh basil (6–8 leaves)
sausage (6 links)
pork neck bone (4–6 pieces)
6 meatballs
2 braciole
½–¾ of water using tomato can
1 can of water from tomato
    paste can

Required pots:
1 large pot

Nonno's tip:
Stir this gravy softly or you'll break
up the sausage and meatballs!

In a large pot on a medium heat,
add sausage, neck bone and
braciole and cook until brown. You
can do one at a time if necessary.
Fry or bake meatballs separately.

Once meat is browned—not
cooked, just browned—remove
from pot and place in a glass bowl.

Using the same pot, add EVOO
and chopped onion and garlic and
reduce to a medium heat.

Sautee for 3 minutes, add salt and
continue scraping the meat from
the bottom.

Add tomato paste and cook for
2–3 minutes, stirring often with a
wooden spoon to prevent burning.

Add tomatoes and continue to mix
and scrape thoroughly.

Bring to a stronger simmer and
add 1 can of water using the
tomato paste can and add some
water from the tomato can to keep
the gravy loose.

Bring to a low heat and simmer for
45 minutes. Continue stirring often,
ensuring that it does not get too
thick as that will cause it to burn.

After simmering, increase the heat
level and add the meat.

Once boiling, reduce down to a
simmer.

Cook for 90 minutes or more, stirring often and softly. Be sure to continue to scrape the bottom as well.

Serve with pasta or ravioli of your choice!

Nonno's great-granddaughter Rachele

Marinara sauce

salsa Marinara

What's the difference between Sunday gravy and Marinara sauce?

As explained by Angelo himself, Sunday gravy is slow cooked for 2–3 hours with or without meat, and Marinara is a quick sauce to cook. Marinaio in Italian means "sailor" and when the sailors used to go into the ports, if the restaurants were out of tomato sauce (aka Sunday gravy) they would make them a "quick" tomato sauce, which is how Marinara Sauce came to get its name.

Qual'è la differenza tra il ragù della domenica e la salsa marinara?

Come Angelo stesso spiegava, il ragù viene cotto lentamente per 2–3 ore, con o senza carne, invece la marinara è una salsa da preparare velocemente. Quando i marinai tornavano in porto, se i ristoranti avevano finito la salsa di pomodoro, facevano loro una versione veloce, che per questo motivo venne chiamata Marinara.

You will need:
1 jar (32 oz) of home canned tomatoes or 1 can (32 oz) of crushed tomatoes
garlic (5–6 cloves; chopped)
½ onion (chopped)
extra virgin olive oil (4–7 second pour)
fresh basil
½ teaspoon or to taste grating cheese

Required pots:
1 medium large pot with lid

Nonno's tip:
Be sure to use good quality grating cheese, no "jarred cheese."

___

With this recipe, 1 jar of tomatoes = 1 lb of pasta

___

Heat EVOO in pot and add chopped garlic and onions. On a medium-high heat, cook until golden brown.

After they start to brown, add salt.

Once golden, add tomatoes (it will splatter so be careful).

Add ⅛ cup water to the tomato jar to pick up leftover residue and pour into sauce.

Add basil (leave some for garnish).

Bring to a boil then reduce to simmer. Cover with lid askew and stir often.

Fill the tomato jar with ¼–½ cup water to use if the sauce gets too thick.

Serve with spaghetti, penne or bowtie pasta (something that holds onto the sauce).

preserving summer

If there is one thing every traditional Italian household knows, it's canning. Canning is a family affair and it's done to provide red sauce and tomatoes until the same time next year. Preserving things was a way of life back then, from sausages to wine. It was such a special day for my sisters and I, because it meant we got to spend the whole day with Nonno and Nonna. Also, if you're friends with any true Italian, you should expect a couple jars as a gift at some point.

Canning is usually done between August and September. In my family, Nonno would take us from place to place to find the best tomatoes. Then we would lay them out on a table for one week to let them ripen and remove any that may have become rotten. Originally, we used old 32 oz glass Coke or Pepsi bottles that we would cap ourselves, until we eventually moved to mason jars.

On the day of canning, the tomatoes would be washed and cut and then we would squish the seeds out by hand then use a hand turn sausage grinder to grind them. Then, Nonno would get the funnels and place them on top of the bottles we were using and take a long stick to push the tomatoes down. He would put basil in halfway through the bottle, fill the rest with tomatoes, and cap it. We would then wrap the bottles with newspaper and place them very tightly into a large vat of water with a potato and cook until the potato was done, which meant the tomatoes were done. Way more efficient than any timer!

After canning was finished, Nonno and Nonna would make us all kinds of treats, my favorite being zucchini pizzetta. There were always mussels prepared, along with pizza made with the tomatoes that were imperfect or that didn't make it into the bottles, for nothing ever went to waste. We would tell stories into the evening, play checkers, and simply enjoy each other's company. These were some of the fondest summer memories for my sisters and I, and the tradition carries on with our families to this day.

Una tradizione per eccellenza propria di ogni famiglia italiana che si rispetti è la conserva fatta in casa. È un affare di famiglia, un antico rito che si ripete di anno in anno, che serve a confezionare la salsa di pomodoro e conservarla per ogni uso culinario fino all'anno seguente. Dalla salsiccia al vino, conservare i prodotti di qualità è sempre stato considerato un vero e proprio stile di vita. Il giorno della conserva era per me e le mie sorelle molto speciale, perché sapevamo che avremmo trascorso l'intera giornata con i nonni. Oltretutto, se hai la fortuna di avere un amico italiano, aspettati di ricevere in dono prima o poi un paio di barattoli di conserva di pomodoro.

Il giorno del grande appuntamento veniva solitamente fissato tra agosto e settembre. Una settimana prima, il nonno ci portava con sé da un posto all'altro per trovare i pomodori dall'aspetto migliore, che avremmo in seguito steso su un tavolo per una settimana a maturare, per poi scartare quelli già marci. Inizialmente, usavamo vecchie bottiglie di Coca Cola o Pepsi che tappavamo noi stessi, fino a quando non passammo ai veri barattoli di vetro.

Il vero e proprio giorno del confezionamento, iniziavamo lavando e tagliando i pomodori, per poi levare i semi a mano e schiacciarli usando un passaverdure. Nel passaggio seguente, il nonno posizionava gli imbuti sopra le bottiglie in uso, per poi prendere un bastoncino lungo che serviva a spingere ben giù i pomodori. A metà della bottiglia aggiungeva il basilico, riempiva il resto con ulteriori pomodori e, per ultimo, avvitava il tappo. Avvolgevamo quindi le bottiglie con del giornale, per poi inserirle una vicina all'altra in una grande tinozza piena d'acqua con una patata, e accendevamo il fuoco fino a quando la patata era ben cotta, a significare che i pomodori erano pronti. Un metodo sicuramente molto più efficace di qualsiasi timer dei nostri tempi!

Una volta concluso il processo di confezionamento, il nonno e la nonna davano il meglio di sé sfornando ogni tipo di delizia, tra le quali puntualmente apparivano le cozze e la mia preferita: la pizzetta di zucchine! Facevano anche la pizza usando le parti dei pomodori imperfetti o non selezionati per

Canning doesn't have to be done in bulk like my family did, which was usually around 3–4 cases. It can literally be just a few jars that you use—with almost any kind of vegetable!

For more information on the canning process, visit *freshpreserving.com/canning-101.html*

la conserva, perchè nulla doveva andare sprecato. Ma non era ancora finita: ci raccontavamo storie fino a sera, giocavamo a dama e, soprattutto, godevamo semplicemente della reciproca compagnia. Queste giornate estive sono per noi fratelli alcuni dei ricordi più preziosi della giovinezza; il pensiero più bello è che questa tradizione di famiglia si tramandi fino ad oggi.

La conserva non dev'essere per forza prodotta in grandi quantità come quelle della mia famiglia—di solito fino a 3–4 contenitori. Si può anche scegliere di riempire pochi barattoli che verranno utilizzati nell'arco dell'anno; inoltre può essere fatta con quasi ogni tipo di verdura!

Pasta with peas—tomato
pasta con piselli e pomodoro

You will need:
**1 can of tomato paste (or home
jarred tomatoes, or 6–8 fresh
plum tomatoes in season)**
**1 can (16 oz) of sweet peas or
2 cups of frozen sweet peas**
½ onion
garlic (6–8 cloves)
**extra virgin olive oil
(3–4 second pour)**
fresh basil
¼ teaspoon of salt
⅛ cup of grating cheese
1 lb of pasta that will hold sauce

Required pots:
1 large (8 quart) pot with lid,
1 medium pot

Nonno's tip:
Canned peas work just fine for
this recipe.

Slice onion and garlic.

Heat EVOO in the large pot, then
add garlic and onion and sauté
over medium–high heat for 2–5
minutes. Add salt and sauté for 2
minutes.

Add tomatoes and basil, bring to a
boil, then reduce to a simmer. Add
water if it becomes too thick.

Add peas (if canned, add ½ the
liquid from the can). Stir and salt
if needed.

Cover with lid askew and let simmer
for 30–40 minutes. Make sure you
check that it doesn't get too thick.

While the sauce is cooking, fill the
medium pot with water and bring
to boil to add pasta.

When the sauce is either finished
or in the last 10 minutes of the
sauce being finished, you can
make the pasta.

Drain the water from the pasta
once it's finished and return the
pasta back to the pot and drizzle
with EVOO.

Start adding the sauce and ½ the
grating cheese to the pasta.

Top with extra sauce and cheese.

PASTA + PEAS
BROWN GARLIC OR ONION WITH A LITTLE
BIT OF OIL THEN ADD ½ CAN DEL MONTE
SAUCE IF YOU HAVE RIPE TOMATOES CUT UP.
ABOUT 3 OR 4 AND COOK THEM AWILE THEN
ADD YOUR CAN OF PEAS SLOWLY COOK
ABOUT 10 OR 15 MIN. THEN COOK YOUR
PASTA YOU COULD USE ELBOW OR CUT UP
SPAGHETTI SMALL PIECES, THEN MIX IT
ITH THE PEAS. YOU COULD ALSO PUT
IN RAW EGGS IN THE PEAS DO NOT
STIR THEM LET THEM STAY WHOLE
ABOUT 1 TO A PERSON ADD SALT

Pasta with peas—white
pasta bianca con piselli

You will need:
fresh peas or 1 can of sweet peas
½ onion
garlic (6–8 cloves)
fresh basil
1 tablespoon grating cheese
  or to taste
¼ cup pancetta
extra virgin olive oil
  (4 second pour)
1 can (16 oz) of peas or 2 cups
  frozen peas
pinch of salt to taste
ditalini pasta

Required pots:
1 medium pot, 1 sauce pan

Nonno's tip:
In this recipe, be generous with the garlic!

Boil water in the pot for your pasta.

In the sauce pan, heat up the EVOO. Add the pancetta and brown.

Slice onion and garlic and add to the pan. Sauté for 3–5 minutes.

Add peas (if canned, add the liquid; if frozen, add 1 cup of water)

Bring to a boil then turn down to simmer.

Once the pasta is done al dente, drain and save about 2–3 cups of water from the pot.

Return pasta back to the pot and put back on the burner on a low heat.

Add sauce and grated cheese to the pasta and stir.

Add the saved pasta water a little at a time until the consistency is loose.

Turn off heat and cover for 3–5 minutes.

Serve with grating cheese on top.

Pasta & fagioli
pasta e fagioli

You will need:
1 can of tomato paste
½ onion (sliced)
garlic (4–8 cloves; sliced)
extra virgin olive oil
  (2–3 second pour)
2–3 cups of white beans, aka
  cannellini (or more if you like)
1 box of ditalini pasta
pinch of salt, then to taste
grating cheese
1 liter of water

Required pots:
1 large pot (6–8 quart)

Nonno's tip:
If possible, use dry beans previously cooked, instead of canned. (See page 24 for a guide to preparing dry beans.)

Heat the EVOO in the pot, then add the onion and garlic. Cook for 5–10 minutes, until lightly brown or translucent.

Add the tomato paste and sauté for 3–5 minutes, stirring regularly to prevent from burning.

Add ½ liter of water and stir so that the paste dissipates in the water.

Bring to boil and let simmer for 20–25 minutes.

After simmering, add beans and bring back to boil.

Reduce heat, let simmer 10 minutes and taste.

How do you know when it's done? When it's not too thick and not too thin—believe me, you'll know!

---

reunited with family

As mentioned earlier, Nonno never returned to his home country after immigrating to the United States in 1921, at just 17 years old. Sadly, he was never able to see his mother or his sister in person again. But we were determined to keep a family connection.

In 1989, I traveled to Italy with my sister because we wanted to finally meet our Neapolitan family. After landing in Europe, my sister and I took the nearly 16 hour train from Germany to Naples and somehow arrived in one piece. Not to age myself but let's just say in 1989 I was a bit younger than I am today and we had a blast on that ride.

When we arrived at my Zio Carlo and Zio Saverio's house, we were greeted with more excitement than I'd ever felt before. I realized not only was

Come accennato in precedenza, una volta arrivato negli Stati Uniti nel 1921 alla sola età di 16 anni, il nonno non fece mai più ritorno nel suo amato paese d'origine. Non aver più messo piede in Italia significò purtroppo non aver mai più rivisto sua sorella e sua mamma. Nonostante ciò, siamo sempre stati molto determinati nel mantenere un forte legame familiare.

Nel 1989, io e mia sorella decidemmo di partire per l'Italia, desiderosi com'eravamo di poter finalmente incontrare la nostra famiglia napoletana. Arrivati in Europa, salimmo su un treno che in ben 16 ore ci portò dalla Germania a Napoli sani e salvi. Non per darmi del vecchio, ma diciamo che nel 1989 ero giusto un tantino più giovane di adesso, e mi ricordo quel viaggio in treno con mia sorella come un divertimento unico.

I seeing my Nonno in my family's faces and mannerisms but they were also seeing him in my sister and I. Even though he wasn't physically there, he was—in a way—because of all of us. We all had that common thread; our Nonno.

After the initial greetings, as per Italian tradition, everyone began to ask us what we wanted to eat and what they could make for us. You'd probably think we would have asked for Ravioli, Lasagne, Braciole, or something along those lines, but we did not. Not even close actually.

Giunti a casa di zio Carlo e zio Saverio, fummo accolti con un ondata di entusiasmo che ci travolse come mai prima. Fu in quel momento che me ne resi davvero conto: proprio come io riconoscevo il caro nonno nei volti e nei comportamenti dei familiari presenti, loro ritrovavano poco a poco le stesse caratteristiche in me e mia sorella. Nonostante non fosse lì fisicamente, in qualche modo la sua presenza era forte in ognuno di noi. Eravamo tutti inevitabilmente legati da un filo che ci teneva ben stretti: nonno Angelo.

We asked for pasta & fagioli and escarole & beans, better known as peasant food. I still remember my Zio Carlo raising an eyebrow to see if perhaps we did not understand what we'd just requested. We all sure got a good laugh out of that and they happily made what we'd asked for, along with about twenty other dishes. Mamma mia, was it good!

Nonno loved to hear that story. It brought him great joy to know that the love of food and cooking still ran strong in his kin. For my sister and I, it was the trip of a lifetime and we will never forget it.

Passato il momento dei saluti iniziali, come da tradizione italiana iniziarono tutti a chiederci cosa gradissimo mangiare e cosa potessero fare per noi. Probabilmente penserete che chiedemmo senza esitazione un piatto di ravioli, lasagne, braciole o qualcosa del genere, ma vi dirò invece che la nostra richiesta fu di tutt'altro genere.

Chiedemmo pasta e fagioli e minestra di scarola e fagioli, classiche pietanze campane. Ricordo ancora l'espressione di mio zio Carlo: sollevò un sopracciglio cercando di capire se per caso non avessimo idea di

cosa fossero veramente quei piatti. La nostra strana richiesta provocò una grande risata generale, ma alla fine furono ben contenti di prepararci i cibi che sognavamo. Insieme ad un'altra ventina di porzioni, ovviamente. Mamma mia se erano buoni!

Il nonno amava ascoltarci raccontare la storia di quel viaggio e di quella particolare giornata. Era così contento di sapere che l'amore per il cibo e la cucina fosse ancora forte e presente nella vita dei suoi parenti napoletani. Per quanto riguarda me e mia sorella, fu semplicemente il viaggio della vita e rimarrà nei nostri cuori per sempre.

Baccala in tomatoes with pasta
pasta con baccalà e pomodori

You will need:
3–4 pieces of baccala (salted cod fish), soaked so it's ready to eat
1 jar homemade tomatoes or 1 can (32 oz) San Marzano tomatoes
garlic (6–8 cloves; whole or sliced)
½ medium onion (chopped; optional)
extra virgin olive oil (2–4 second pour)
fresh basil (8–10 leaves)
pinch of salt

Required pots:
1 large frying pan, 1 large pot

Nonno's tip:
Remember baccala is cured cod fish, so once it has been rehydrated it does not have to be cooked.

Heat up EVOO in a large frying pan and add baccalla, browning lightly. Once heated through, place on a dish.

In the same pan, add EVOO then the garlic and onion and sauté lightly.

Add tomatoes and basil and cook for 10–12 minutes until the water is almost gone. Pre-heat oven to 350° to warm up while that cooks.

Add bacalla back into pan, cover with lid or foil and place in the oven for 20 minutes.

While that is cooking, start boiling water for pasta so they can both be ready around the same time.

Once everything is finished, remove baccala from the pan and use the tomato mixture to sauce the pasta.

Fried baccala
baccalà fritto

You will need:
3–4 pieces of baccala (salted cod fish), soaked so it's ready to eat
flour for coating
extra virgin olive oil (⅛ cup)

Required pots:
1 frying pan

Nonno's tip:
I always like to have a side of fried peppers with my fried baccala.

Use a shallow dish to pour flour in to dredge baccala.

Pour EVOO into the frying pan so that it covers the bottom and heat at medium level.

Once the EVOO is hot, add baccala and fry until brown (the baccala is cured so as soon as its golden brown it's done).

Serve hot, warm or cold.

103   Nonno with his brother in-laws and friends Francine, Dominic, Jimmy, Ida and Charlie, Tony and Marie

You will need:
**1 pizza dough (homemade or
    from pizzeria)**
**1 can (32 oz) of crushed tomatoes
    (or home jarred)**
**extra virgin olive oil
    (2–4 second pours)**
garlic (6 cloves; quartered)
¼–½ grating cheese
4–6 basil leaves
½ teaspoon salt
**8 oz mozzarella (fresh or
    packaged; grated or sliced)**
**flour (for surface when kneading
    and stretching dough)**

Required pots:
1 baking sheet

Nonno's tip:
This is also tasty without the
mozzarella and just grating cheese.

Preheat oven to 450°.

On a floured surface, stretch dough
to roughly the size of a baking sheet.

Drizzle EVOO in the baking sheet
and move around with your hands
to ensure the whole pan and sides
are covered.

Fit dough in a baking sheet so that
it slightly comes over the sides.

Add garlic and salt to the tomatoes
and stir with a ladle or spoon and
spread so that there is a thin layer
of tomatoes (so it's transparent in
some areas and not in other areas).

Sprinkle a light dusting of grating
cheese, EVOO and ripped basil
leaves.

Bake until the crust starts to
brown, about 10–15 min.

Remove and add mozzarella, then
place back in the oven until the
crust is brown.

OLMC feast

The OLMC Feast, also known as Our Lady of Mount Carmel, is now part of the traditions of our family, thanks to Nonno Angelo. The feast takes place in Williamsburg, Brooklyn, the neighborhood in which Nonno used to hang out with other southern Italian immigrants from his same region when he first arrived in the USA. It started over 100 years ago and continues to this day.

The feast is always held sometime in early July. Now, if you've ever been to New York in July, you know chances are it's going to be hot, and if you haven't been, imagine sitting in a pizza oven while wearing wool. Nevertheless, the heat never stopped my family from packing up the car and making the pilgrimage to Brooklyn. No one

La festa di Nostra Signora del Monte Carmelo, in inglese denominata "OLMC Feast", fa parte ormai delle tradizioni della nostra famiglia, proprio grazie a nonno Angelo. Dopo oltre cent'anni di festeggiamenti, ha ancora luogo ogni anno a Williamsburg, Brooklyn, Il quartiere in cui il nonno era solito passare il tempo con altri immigrati provenienti dalla sua stessa regione d'Italia, nei primi tempi della sua nuova vita americana.

La celebrazione si svolge sempre all'inizio di luglio. Se sei mai stato a New York nel mese di luglio, sai bene il caldo che potrebbe esserci, se non ci sei stato immagina semplicemente di sederti in un forno da pizza mentre indossi vestiti di lana: ci si sente proprio così! Le elevate temperature, tuttavia, non scoraggiarono mai la mia famiglia a caricare la macchina e iniziare il pellegrinaggio con destinazione Brooklyn. Nessuno avrebbe mai osato lamentarsi del caldo, siccome tutti sapevano bene quanto fosse importante questa festa per il nonno.

Con mia nonna Rose sulla sedia a rotelle, dovevamo organizzarci per arrivare molto presto e riuscire ad ottenere un buon posto tra le prime file per la parata. Ricordo come da ragazzo osservassi con ammirazione la totale protezione che il nonno aveva nei confronti della nonna, nel mezzo della grande folla. La teneva d'occhio tutto il tempo, assicurandosi che nessuno le andasse addosso o le si avvicinasse troppo, mentre lei si godeva la festa ed esultava dalla sua sedia a rotelle. Ai miei occhi era una scena commovente, perché mi rendevo conto già da bambino che lui per la nonna avrebbe fatto qualunque cosa. Nonostante fosse fisicamente piuttosto minuto, il nonno in quei momenti mi sembrava davvero un gigante.

L'emozione negli occhi del nonno cresceva durante la preparazione della Torre del Giglio e l'inizio delle musiche: ricordo che, ogni volta, osservavo senza dire niente le lacrime che scorrevano lungo il suo viso. Crescendo, mi sono reso conto che questa festa era ciò che di più vicino a casa sua mio nonno avesse, e l'unico modo per sentirsi in connessione con la sua famiglia e il paese in cui era nato. Poter trascorrere la giornata e festeggiare con vecchi amici e conoscenti che condividevano la sua cultura e l'amore per la patria d'origine era per lui un regalo immenso.

Nella famiglia Iovine, la tradizione di partecipare annualmente all' "OLMC Feast" continua ancora oggi, e io mi commuovo ogni volta al pensiero che il nonno non possa essere presente lì con noi. Ne sarebbe immensamente orgoglioso. Non dimenticheremo mai le sue origini e la sua storia.

dared complaining about the heat, because everyone knew how much Nonno enjoyed the celebration.

With my Nonna Rose being in a wheelchair, we would arrive extra early to get a good spot up front for the parade. I remember as a boy observing the fierce protectiveness Nonno had over Nonna in the large crowd. He kept a watchful eye on her, ensuring no one ran into her or got too close, as she cheered on from her wheelchair. It was so touching because even as a kid I knew he would do anything for my Nonna. Even though he wasn't physically a very big guy, he seemed huge in those moments to me.

As the lift would get ready and the music would start, you could see the buildup in my Nonno's emotions. I remember looking up at him and seeing tears roll down his cheeks but I never said anything. As I got older, I realized this festival was the closest thing my Nonno had to his home in Italy and was the closest he would ever be again to his family and the village where he was born. For him, to be around old friends and acquaintances that share his culture and celebrating all of it, that was a treasure.

The yearly tradition of going to the OLMC Feast carries on in the Iovine family. I've definitely shed a couple tears thinking about my Nonno not being there with us for the event, I know he would be proud. We will never forget his journey and where he came from.

Mussels
cozze

You will need:
2–3 lbs of mussels
½–1 cup of water
fresh parsley
32 oz marinara sauce
water

Depending on the mussels you get, soak them and debeard if necessary.

Required pots:
1 large pot with lid

Nonno's tip:
Cultured mussels are easier to prepare, and you will not have to let them soak or debeard.

In large pot, place mussels and add water to make sure it covers the bottom.

Cover and heat on a high temperature.

When you see the steam start to escape, check and stir.

When the mussels are open ¼–½ way, add ½ of the marinara sauce and cover for another 3–4 minutes.

Once the all the mussels have opened fully, they are finished cooking. The mussels that do not open should not be eaten.

Pour out liquid from the pot and add the remaining marinara sauce and fresh parsley.

Nonno and Nonna with their son Francesco and daughter-in-law Barbara

**Baked chicken with garlic
and parsley**
pollo al forno con aglio
e prezzemolo

You will need:
**1 chicken, cut up (you can use
thighs and legs if you wish)
garlic (4–8 cloves, halved or
quartered)
fresh parsley
4–6 potatoes (peeled)
1 can of peas or 1–1½ cup of
frozen peas
extra virgin olive oil
(4–6 second pour, twice)
2 pinches of salt**

Required pots:
1 large roasting pan

Nonno's tip:
This meal works great family style
or individually plated.

Heat oven to 350°.

Put chicken in roasting pan and
rub and coat with EVOO and salt.

Stuff 2–3 pieces of garlic and some
parsley under the chicken skin.

Coat the potatoes with EVOO and
salt and spread them out in the pan.

Cover with foil and cook for 30
minutes. Chicken will start to
shrink to the bone and some skin
will brown.

Uncover (keep the foil) and cook
for 15–20 minutes, checking
throughout.

Add peas about 10 minutes into
cooking (you can add the
water too).

Check to make sure chicken is finished in whatever method you like.

Once done, cover back up and let
sit until ready to serve.

the hat

"For no matter what the world, men who deal in headwear are men to be trusted above any other."
Frank Beddor

Nonno was most certainly a man who wore many hats, figuratively and literally. As evident through this book, Nonno was a true jack-of-all-trades and could perform just about any task. He would never leave the house without wearing a hat, no matter where he was going.

"Cascasse il mondo, gli uomini che fanno affari indossando cappelli sono uomini di cui fidarsi più di tutti gli altri."
Frank Beddor

Nonno Angelo era un uomo che indossava sicuramente molti cappelli, sia in senso figurato che letterale. Come risulta evidente dai racconti di questo libro, era un vero e proprio tuttofare; qualunque attività ci fosse da svolgere o problema da risolvere, era in grado di occuparsene fino in fondo. Non sarebbe mai e poi mai uscito di casa senza indossare un capello, ovunque stesse andando.

Spaghetti "garlic & oil"
spaghetti aglio olio

You will need:
1 lb spaghetti or angel hair pasta
garlic (6–8 cloves; chopped or
**   sliced)**
¼ cup extra virgin olive oil
parsley
1 jar of anchovies (optional)
4–8 each of walnuts & hazelnuts,
**   shelled (optional)**

Required pots:
1 saucepan, 1 large pot

Nonno's tip:
Anchovies aren't always everyone's favorite, but they really enhance the flavors of this sauce so well!

In a saucepan, heat the EVOO and just before simmering, turn off and add garlic and nuts. They should start to brown (if cooking too fast, add more oil to cool down).

Cook pasta as desired and, when draining, reserve 3–4 cups of water in a separate container.

Once pasta is drained, drizzle EVOO to prevent it from sticking together.

Very important—do not use hot EVOO in this next step:

Add ½ the anchovies to the pan with EVOO and nuts that has cooled down, and add 1 cup pasta water, stirring constantly. Add more water if necessary.

Put on a low heat and let cook, stirring often.

Once the anchovies have cooked (they disappear), add ¼ of sauce to the pasta and gently heat up.

Once heated through, place in a serving dish and pour the rest of the sauce of top.

Top with anchovies and sprinkle with parsley.

Pasta and potatoes
pasta e patate

You will need:
**your choice of marinara sauce,
    sunday gravy (no meat), tomato
    paste or fresh tomatoes**
**3–4 potatoes (peeled and cooked;
    reserve ½–1 cup cooking water)**
garlic (4–6 cloves; sliced)
1 small onion (chopped)
**cooked pasta of choice (elbow,
    ditalini, broken spaghetti)**
**extra virgin olive oil
    (3–4 second pour)**
salt to taste

Required pots:
3 pots—1 for cooking potatoes,
1 for sauce (if not using already
made), 1 for pasta (which will be
the finishing pot)

Nonno's tip:
Try this filling dish with each kind of
sauce and find out which you prefer!

Heat EVOO in pan and sauté
garlic and onion.

Take tomato sauce of choice; add
garlic and onion and mix.

Add reserved potato water to
loosen up sauce (except if using
tomato paste).

Let simmer for 5–10 minutes, then
add potatoes.

Return to a boil, add cooked pasta
and stir until fully mixed and heated.

Turn off heat and cover with lid
for 5 minutes before serving.

Savoy cabbage
verza

You will need:
½ **cabbage head (roughly cut)**
garlic (2–6 cloves, sliced)
½ **onion**
extra virgin olive oil
  (3–4 second pour)
¼–½ **cup of water**
red pepper flakes (optional)
salt to taste

Required pots:
1 medium size pot

Nonno's tip:
When your sense of smell starts to pick up the aroma of all the ingredients melding with a sweet note, that means the cabbage is almost finished!

Heat EVOO in pot on medium heat and lightly brown garlic and onion.

Add salt and wait a minute.

Add cabbage and water, enough to coat the bottom of the pot.

Cover and decrease to a low heat.

In 5–10 minutes, the cabbage will start to soften. The most common length of time to cook is between 20–30 min, but that varies between one's texture preferences.

Add optional hot red pepper flakes just before the dish is finished. If you add it prior, your whole dish will be hot.

You can also add soppressata sweet sausage to this dish by sautéing it with the garlic and onion.

Minestra
(Nonno's classic Italian stew)
minestra

If you asked Nonno to make a minestra, he would ask, "Are you sure you don't want spaghetti?" He'd try to talk you into something quicker to make because minestra took half the morning to make and Nonno only had four pots so it was quite time consuming. But, Nonno wasn't one to say no to those he loved so he would always grant our wish, even if it included a few annoyed huffs and puffs on the way to the kitchen.

Ogni volta che qualcuno di noi chiedeva al nonno di preparare la minestra, lui rispondeva: "Ma sei proprio sicuro di non volere un bel piatto di spaghetti?". Cercava di convincerci in ogni modo a chiedere qualcos'altro, qualunque altro piatto fuorché quello, perché sapeva che per preparare la minestra avrebbe impiegato più di mezza mattinata. Inoltre, il nonno aveva solamente quattro pentole, quindi la preparazione richiedeva ancora più tempo. Tuttavia, non era proprio il tipo di persona da dire di no ai suoi cari, quindi alla fine esaudiva sempre il nostro desiderio, nonostante lo sentissimo sbuffare di tanto in tanto in cucina. Una cosa è sicura, ne valeva sempre la pena!

You will need:
1 head of savoy cabbage
escarole
chicory
celery (4–5 stalks; sliced)
1 onion (sliced)
garlic (4–8 cloves; sliced)
prosciutto end with bone in (ham hock can be substituted if needed)
½ hot & sweet soppressata or dried sausage
⅛–¼ cup of extra virgin olive oil
1 teaspoon salt to taste
water (⅔ of the pot used)
2–3 cups of cooked white beans (optional)
kale (optional)

Thoroughly wash the cabbage, escarole, chicory, celery, and kale to rid it of any dirt or sand.

Required pots:
1 large or extra large pot with lid

Nonno's tip:
Halve the onions for a more simple slicing experience.

Cut or rip the washed cabbage, escarole, chicory, celery, and kale—there is no right or wrong way to cut.

Add chopped cabbage, escarole, chicory, celery, and kale to pot along with prosciutto or ham hock.

Fill pot with approximately ⅔ cup water and add salt and pour in ⅛–¼ cup EVOO (I usually count to 10 for the right amount).

Place pot on high heat.

Add sliced onions and garlic and add to the pot. Cover with lid.

Slice the dried meat in ½ the long way then slice into smaller pieces. Make sure not to slice it too thin.

Add all the ingredients to the pot and mix.

Bring water to a boil, then slow simmer for 2–3 hours, topping up on water when needed.

How do you know when it's done? The aroma of the meats and vegetables will meld when the vegetables have absorbed the meats oils!

Sausage and peppers
salsiccia e peperoni

You will need:
Italian sausage (6–8 links, cut into 3–4 pieces)
6 bell peppers (sliced into ¼ inch pieces; you can add more peppers if you like)
4–5 vinegar peppers, aka pepper hulls★
8–10 onions ("french cut")
garlic (9 cloves; halved or quartered)
extra virgin olive oil (¼ cup)
1 tablespoon salt
hot cherry peppers (optional)

★ Pepper hulls are raw red peppers that are marinated in vinegar, not to be confused with roasted red peppers. They contain vinegar and salt, not oil.

Required pots:
1 roasting pan

Nonno's tip:
The peppers and onion mixture in this recipe can be cooked a day or two in advance to make this a simple weeknight meal.

Heat oven to 450°.

In a roasting pan, combine onion, garlic, salt and ½ EVOO and mix. In a second pan place the peppers and rest of the EVOO.

Place in the oven for about 20–30 minutes, until the edges of the onions begin to brown, and the peppers are soft. Stir occasionally, cook until they are cooked through, soft and slightly brown; longer if you prefer. After 30 minutes you will have to watch them both, to obtain the texture you prefer of each item. Once you have that you can combine them both into the same pan to meld flavors.

Add a some of liquid from the jar of vinegar peppers. This is a taste thing so my suggestion is to start with ¼ of the liquid the first time you make the dish, then add more if you want.

Once cooked, remove vegetables from the oven and let cool.

In a separate pan, add sausage with some water to cover the bottom of the sausage. Place in the oven and bake for around 30–40 minutes.

When sausage is done, add the pepper mix to the pan, cover with foil and heat through, 10–15 minutes.

Serve with bread or as a sandwich!

Sausage, potatoes and peas
salsiccia, patate e piselli

As kids, we would fight over the potatoes that stuck to the pan in this classic recipe.

You will need:
Italian sausage (6–8 links)
potatoes (3–6, peeled)
1 can (16 oz) peas, or 1–1½ cups frozen peas
garlic (6–8 cloves, halved)
1 onion (sliced)
extra virgin olive oil (4–6 second pour)
¼ teaspoon salt

Required pots:
1 roasting pan

Heat oven to 350°.

In roasting pan, add potatoes, garlic and onion.

Add EVOO and salt so that everything is coated.

Spread out sausage links throughout the pan.

Bake for 20–30 minutes, then stir potatoes to prevent sticking (some still will) and cook for another 10 minutes.

Add the peas and cover with foil.

Reduce heat to 200°, making sure it doesn't get overcooked.

Cook for another 30–45 minutes, then cover with foil to keep moist.

checkers

Nonno knew the importance of mental health as well as exercise, and kept fit in several ways. There weren't many times that you'd catch him just sitting around unless of course it was to soak his feet at the end of the day. He would spend a great deal of time at the Belmont Race Track, walking to and from, to keep his brain stimulated, as well as his social life. Nonno's passion for gardening helped keep him focused and being present in the moment.

One of my favorite memories of Nonno's mental sharpness took place when I was about 12 or 13 years old. Nonno was an expert checkers player and he played with purpose to expand his mental ability. Like when playing checkers, every move he made in life was with intention.

So, I go over to Nonno's house and I see him in the backyard with one of his neighbors. This was a daily thing as he and his neighbors often exchanged gardening tips or any other advice they could give one another. But this time I saw them making movements with their hands and noticed that they weren't speaking to each other. I asked him what they were doing and he told me they were playing checkers. I blinked a few times times because I didn't see any board or checker pieces. When he saw my confusion, Nonno pointed to his head and said:

"We are playing in our minds. We have the board and pieces up here."

I was absolutely astonished at this very concept. I couldn't believe that something like that was even possible. Yet, Nonno and his neighbor continued their mental checkers game that day and many more days in the future. That day I knew for sure that Nonno had become my absolute idol.

Nonno Angelo è sempre stato consapevole dell'importanza tanto della salute mentale come di quella fisica, il che lo spronava a mantenersi in forma in diversi modi. Non capitava quasi mai di trovarlo seduto a far niente, eccetto le volte in cui metteva i piedi a mollo a fine giornata. Per stimolare la mente e la vita sociale, trascorreva gran parte del suo tempo libero a fare avanti e indietro dalla pista da corsa di Belmont. Oltre a questo, la sua grande passione per il giardinaggio lo aiutava molto a tenere allenata la concentrazione e ad essere presente nel momento.

A proposito della sua acutezza mentale, uno dei miei ricordi preferiti del nonno risale a quando avevo circa 12 o 13 anni. Da esperto giocatore di dama qual era, aveva come scopo principale quello di migliorare le sue capacità mentali. Proprio come nella dama, ogni mossa che faceva nella vita era pienamente intenzionale.

Un giorno, recatomi a casa del nonno, lo vidi in giardino con uno dei vicini. Non che ne fossi sorpreso: trovarsi tra vicini era un'abitudine quotidiana, in quanto si scambiavano spesso consigli sul giardinaggio o su qualunque altro argomento riguardo il quale si potessero aiutare a vicenda. Tuttavia, quella volta li intravidi fare dei movimenti con le mani e notai che non stavano parlando. Chiesi cosa stessero facendo e mi rispose che stavano giocando a dama. Ne rimasi alquanto sorpreso, non vedendo nessuna scacchiera né tantomeno pedine. Accortosi della mia confusione, il nonno si indicò la testa e disse: "Stiamo giocando nelle nostre menti. Quassù abbiamo la scacchiera e tutte le pedine necessarie".

Rimasi a bocca aperta, non riuscivo neanche ad immaginare come fosse possibile giocare a dama nella mente. Eppure, il nonno e il vicino continuarono il loro gioco mentale come se niente fosse, e da quel giorno mi capitò di trovarli nella stessa situazione molte altre volte. Che dire, se non lo era già da prima, da quel giorno nonno Angelo è diventato il mio idolo assoluto.

Share Meals and Memories of your own and join Nonno's online community on our website!
www.mealsandmemorieswithnonno.com

Swiss chard, sausage & potato
bietola, salsiccia e patate

You will need:
1 bunch of swiss chard
garlic (4–6 cloves)
extra virgin olive oil
  (4 second pours, twice)
sausage (4–6 links)
3–4 potatoes (cut into quarters)
½ teaspoon of salt
½ cup of water

Required pots:
1 small pot, 1 roasting pan

Nonno's tip:
Swiss chard, like spinach and kale, will shrink in size tremendously when it's cooked, so be generous with how much you use!

Preheat oven to 350°.

Wash and rinse swiss chard and trim stems by cutting where the stems end and the leaves begin.

Cut stems into 3 inch pieces and place in small pot of water, boiling until tender.

Cut swiss chard leaves and potatoes and coat with 1 pour of EVOO and a pinch of salt (you can do this in the roasting pan).

Place all the ingredients into the roasting pan, drizzle with EVOO and add water.

Cover and cook in oven for 30 minutes. Check to see if sausage and potatoes are turning brown, then uncover and cook for 10 more minutes.

Swiss chard stems with eggs
steli di bietole con uova

You will need:
4–6 swiss chard stems (boiled)
4 eggs (beaten)
extra virgin olive oil
  (4 second pour)
pinch of salt

Required pots:
1 sauté pan

Nonno's tip:
Swiss chard stems are filled with
nutrients so make sure to use them!

Place boiled swiss chard stems into
pan with EVOO and sauté for 5
minutes.

Add beaten eggs and cook like an
omelet.

Add a pinch of salt before serving.

Roasted nuts
noci tostate

You will need:
1 lb of filberts, walnuts, almonds or brazil nuts

Required pots:
1 baking sheet used only for nuts

Nonno's tip:
Each nut has a different roasting point. Roast separately for best results.

Heat over to 450°.

In a baking sheet, add nuts and cook for 3 minutes.

Move nuts around with a spoon.

In 2–3 minute intervals, shake the pan or stir with spoon until you can start to smell them.

Once you have the aroma, remove from the oven and place in a cooling bowl (if it's cold outside you can place outside to cool).

Have fun with it and if you burn some just try again!

129

Escarole pie
pizza di scarola

You will need:

2 heads of escarole or chicory, well cleaned
¾ of a ring of dried figs
½ cup of raisins
¼ cup of pine nuts
12 green olives (pitted & cut up)
half of a 2–3 oz container of anchovies
12 filberts nuts, shelled and broken up
6 walnuts, shelled and broken up
2 delicious apples (cut up)
⅛–¼ cup citron (more if you like)
extra virgin olive oil (2–3 second pour for the escarole)
pie crust (store bought or homemade)★

Nonno's tip:
This recipe was one that we generally made around Christmas time.

Heat oven to 350°.

Steam the escarole with EVOO until tender and remove from the pot, leaving the juices in the pot.

Add the rest of the ingredients except the escarole to the pot with the juices and cook until all the liquid has evaporated.

Once cooled, add the escarole to the other ingredients and mix together.

In a separate pan, add the bottom layer of the pie crust.

Put some of the escarole on the bottom of the pie crust and then add some of the other mix. Do this pattern until the pan is almost full, then the rest of the escarole and ingredients to the pie crust.

Add the other pie crust to the top of the mixture and brush with milk or beaten eggs.

Cut slits in the top for steam and bake until golden brown (between 35–50 minutes depending on oven).

Serve cold or warm!

★ Try your own Nonna's holiday pie crust recipe, or take a look at the following page!

Pie Crust Recipe

Courtesy of the old fashioned Crisco recipe from the back of the bottle (which we used sometimes).

You will need:
2 ⅔ C. all-purpose flour
1 tsp. salt
1 C. cold Crisco® all-vegetable shortening or 6 to 10 tbsps.
ice cold water

Heat oven to 350°.

Stir flour and salt in large bowl until blended. Cut shortening into flour mixture using pastry blender or fork until shortening pieces are the size of peas. Gradually add just enough water, 1 tbsp. at a time, stirring with fork just until dough holds together and forms a smooth ball.

Shape dough into a ball for single pie crust. Divide dough in half and shape into two balls for double crust pie. Leave in ball or flatten into ½-inch thick disk(s). Wrap ball / disk(s) in plastic wrap. Chill 30 minutes or up to 2 days.

Roll dough on lightly floured surface, rolling from center outward. For 9-inch pie plate, roll into an 11-inch circle. For 9 ½-inch deep-dish pie plate, roll into a 12-inch circle. Transfer dough to pie plate.

For Single-Crust pie, fold edge under and press to form a standing rim. Flute edge as desired. Chill until ready to use.

For Double-Crust pie, roll disk for bottom crust, trimming edges of dough even with outer edge of pie plate. Fill unbaked pie crust according to recipe directions. Roll out remaining dough disk. Place dough over filled pie crust. Trim edges of dough leaving a ¾-inch overhang. Fold top edge under bottom crust. Press edges together to seal. Flute edges as desired. Cut several ½-inch slits in top crust to vent steam. Bake according to specific recipe directions.

INTER-OFFICE COMMUNICATION

	FROM	DATE
aza Ca Escarole Made at Christmas time.		
	RE	

carole Steam with some oil. 2 heads of curly escarole the outside aves until soft. Take out of pot let juice stay to the bottom of t then add to the pot with the juice in.

4 string of figs cut up small
up of raisins, ¼ cup pignola 12 Green olives cut up small
box anchovies 12 Filberts broken up 6 walnuts broken up
deliciousapples cup up some citron or a half of a whole citron.

eam all ingredients until juice is used up. When cooled off d escarole and ingredients to a two crust pie dough 0 degree oven.

t some escarole on bottom of pie crust then other ingredients en some more escarole the n put on top pie crust close tighly gether make some holes on top for air. Then brush some milk top

in dough — regular pie crust.

132   Nonno's great-great nephews Daniele and Luca

Kale with garlic
cavolo riccio con aglio

You will need:
1 bunch of kale
garlic (4–6 cloves; sliced or
  quartered)
½ teaspoon of salt
extra virgin olive oil
  (4–6 second pour)
½–1 cup of water

Required pots:
1 large pot

Nonno's tip:
This dish can be eaten hot or cold
or added to bigger recipes as well.

Wash kale thoroughly, trim the bottoms and place kale into a large pot.

Add garlic, salt, EVOO, and water, enough to cover the bottom of the pot, about ½ inch.

Bring to a boil and then reduce to a simmer, topping up the water level often.

Cook until kale is tender, about 10–15 minutes.

"20 going on 19"

My family has always been very big on birthday parties and that's definitely because of Nonno. It brought him so much happiness to have everyone together celebrating life and watching his kids, grandkids and great-grandkids grow another year older. After all nothing is guaranteed, as Nonno knew through his life experience.

Whenever it was his birthday and someone asked how old he was turning, he'd always say, "20 going on 19." We knew he was going to say it every time but still asked it each year and he would never miss a beat. More so, it was truly funny every time he said it too.

Aside from the yearly prank cardboard-cake he would make for Nonna, Nonno could bake all kinds of delicious things, but it was my Nonna Rose who was the official baker, famously known for her white cake. Between the two of them, every birthday we had was perfect.

I compleanni sono sempre stati eventi di grande importanza nella mia famiglia, soprattutto grazie all'entusiasmo che il nonno dimostrava ogni volta durante i festeggiamenti. Essere riuniti tutti assieme per celebrare la vita e osservare i propri figli, nipoti e bisnipoti crescere di anno in anno era per lui motivo di gioia immensa. Dopotutto, come il nonno ben sapeva in virtù della sua esperienza, nella vita non c'è mai nulla di certo.

In occasione del suo compleanno, ogni volta che qualcuno gli chiedeva quanti anni compisse, la sua risposta era sempre la stessa: "19!". Pur consapevoli che la sua età fittizia non sarebbe cambiata, ogni anno noi nipoti ci presentavamo con la fatidica domanda, e non c'era volta in cui non si lasciasse scappare l'occasione di ripetere convinto lo stesso numero. La verità è che morivamo dal ridere ogni volta che glielo sentivamo ripetere.

A parte lo scherzo della torta di cartone che faceva ogni anno per la nonna Rose, il nonno si dava un gran daffare ad infornare ogni tipo di dolce sfizioso, nonostante la vera professionista dei dolci fosse proprio la nonna Rose, la cui più grande specialità era la "torta bianca". Insomma, grazie alla compagnia del nonno e della nonna, ognuno dei nostri compleanni trascorsi insieme era semplicemente perfetto.

White cake
torta bianca

Nonna Rose was the baker in the family and no one was better than her.

Nonna Rose era indiscutibimente la miglior pasticcera della famiglia.

You will need:
1 cup Fluffo (or Crisco)
2 cups sugar
1 cup milk
2 ¾ cup flour
2 tsp baking powder
2 tsp vanilla
1 tsp salt
4 eggs

Nonno's tip:
Everyone in the family has tried to reproduce this cake and find it very difficult to make without the Fluffo.

Cream sugar and Fluffo

Add eggs and mix together.

Blend in flour, salt, baking powder, milk and vanilla.

Heat oven to 350°.

Check in 20 minutes with toothpick. Cook until finished.

White cake
1 cup fluffo
2cups sugar
1 cup milk
2 3/4 cup flour

3 teasp. baking power
2 teasp. vanilla
1 teasp. salt
4 eggs

cream sugar & fluffo. add eggs, mix. Blend in flour,salt, baking powder alternately with milk and

Migliaccio cake
torta migliaccio

This cake is a form of Neapolitan cake and specific to the region of Italy where Nonno is from. Traditionally, it was made for the day before Ash Wednesday, and only eaten this time of year. Nonno would do a type of intermittent fasting where he would only eat this in the morning and nothing else until the following morning.

Questa è una torta napoletana, tipica della zona da cui viene il nonno. Tradizionalmente si faceva il giorno prima del mercoledì delle Ceneri, giorno di digiuno per i cattolici praticanti. Nonno mangiava solo una fetta di questa torta per colazione e poi nient'altro fino al giorno seguente.

You will need:
1 cup farina/semolina flour
2 quarts milk (or 4 cups)
¼ pound of butter (or 1 stick)
2 cups sugar
2 tangerine skins, diced or grated
  (or 1 lemon skin grated)
12 eggs
1 tablespoon vanilla extract
  (optional)

Nonno's tips:
For a smaller version of this recipe, use half-portion of the above ingredients.

This recipe calls for a large amount of sugar, you can adjust that if you please. You can also substitute regular milk with unsweetened almond milk.

In a pot, bring milk to boil.

Add farina/semolina flour (a little at a time), sugar, sliced butter and vanilla. Let cool.

Beat eggs and add tangerine skins.

Mix 2–3 cups of the warm mix with the eggs to temper them, then mix all together thoroughly.

Grease cake pan with butter and sprinkle dry farina/semolina flour on the bottom.

Pour mixture into pan and add 3–4 dabs of butter to the top spacing them apart from each other.

Heat oven to 350° and cook until the top is brown, about 45 minutes.

Cake for the day
before Ash Wednesday

½ box of Farina
small box
2 qts milk
¼ lb. butter
2 cups sugar
2 skins cut ups of
tangerines or
lemon rind

the gas let it cool
awhile then put in
beaten eggs +
Tangerine skins
+ mix together
put butter on bottom
of pan with some
farina sprinkled
around then put
cooked Farina then
on Top put dabs
butter on top ba

famiglia dinner 2021

This past August (2021), I traveled to Italy for my cousin Daniele's wedding and what an amazing time I had! I was able to speak and spend time with my family and Nonno's niece Rafaelina and her husband Giovanni whom I had not seen since 2016. Despite the years that had passed since we'd all been together, everything fell right into place as it does with those you love.

This gave me the opportunity to take a chance just like my Nonno did in 1921. Ok maybe not that big of a chance but you tell me! I was able to prepare five of the recipes from this book for my family in their home. Basically it felt like having Leonardo Da Vinci judge your painting and needless to say my nerves were exeptionally high.

All I know was that Napoletano was being spoken, so it quickly reminded me of being at my Nonno's and Nonna's, when family was over and I was younger. The only thing I could pick up was that the food I cooked brought them back to Naples and that was the highest praise I could've dreamed of. It was the most energetic and the loudest sense of peace I've felt in a long time.

Of course, it's always better in their words. The following message was sent to me after my recent visit from Rafaelina and Giovanni (translated by my cousin Luca):

Quant'è bell stà tutt'insieme
in grazia e Dio intorno a tavola
innanz a nu piatt e pasta.

How beautiful it is to be all together
In peace and love around the table
In front of a plate of pasta

Pure se stamm allatra part ro munn,
u sang buon nu mente mai
e i piatt e Frank parlano a stessa lengua nostra,
u NAPOLETANO.

Although we are in the other side of the world
blood can never lie
And Frank's plates speak our same language,
The NAPOLETANO

E come se dice:
A meglia mericina:
vino e campagna,
purpette e cucina.

And how we're used to say:
The best medicine:
Wine and fields,
Meatballs and cooking
(without rhyme is not so beautiful)

Grazie assaje Frank.
Many thanks Frank.

For all your Italian specialties and imports.
2147 Jericho Turnpike
Garden City, NY 11040

sansonemarketgardencity.com

For fruits and vegetables.
246 Hempstead Ave
Lynbrook, NY 11563

crossislandfruits.net

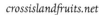

About the author

Franceso Iovine was born and raised in NYC where food has always been a huge part of his upbringing and life. His love for cuisine started when he was very young in his Nonno and Nonna's kitchen and continued to grow when he started working in a German deli owned by a man named Bruno, a chef who escaped from East Germany. Bruno taught him how to use a knife and everything else was self-taught by observing his grandparents and others who specialize in Italian regional cooking.

Franceso developed his own style of cooking by using his senses, such as taste and smell, as they are more important than the sense of sight when it comes to food and eating. Ask yourself; does a blind person not know what tastes good? The sense of smell tells you what's quality!

Presentation has a lot to do with the final step of preparing a meal but it can also impede you. If you prepare a dish and it doesn't match the photo you were trying to follow, you may tell yourself it won't taste good when it could actually be delicious. That's why we intentionally did not include any photos of the final dish in this book and only the ingredients.

Allora, Franceso wants you to enjoy the recipes in this book to the fullest extent by using your sense of smell and taste. Use your sense of sight mainly so you don't cut your fingers off and so you don't miss your mouth trying to eat. Yes, we eat with our eyes but as Francesco says it's only to make sure the food gets in his mouth so he can taste it.

Buon appetito!
Francesco

We hope you enjoyed "Meals and Memories with Nonno"!

Continuing with Nonno's humanitarian spirit, a portion of the sales from this book will be donated to charity.

Be sure to check out Nonno's online community and share your own meals and memories for a chance to be featured in our next book.
You can also cook along with Frank at: *mealsandmemorieswithnonno.com*

Go forward and conquer!
Alla nostra salute!

colophon

Meals and Memories with Nonno

Published by Gatekeeper Press
2167 Stringtown Rd, Suite 109
Columbus, OH 43123-2989
www.GatekeeperPress.com

Library of Congress Control Number: 2022930645
ISBN (hardcover): 9781662921841
ISBN (paperback): 9781662927034
eISBN: 9781662921858

Text: Francesco Iovine & Ashley Carr
Editing: Ashley Carr
Translations: Luisa Buzzi

Design: Margherita Buzzi
Typeset in Dante MT
Cover design: Damion James Tedeschi

All photos are from the Iovine's family albums,
scanned by Michael Tolani and Loupe Digital.
Artichoke & tangerine photos by Danny Pham

For more information visit our website or email:
www.mealsandmemorieswithnonno.com
info@mealsandmemorieswithnonno.com

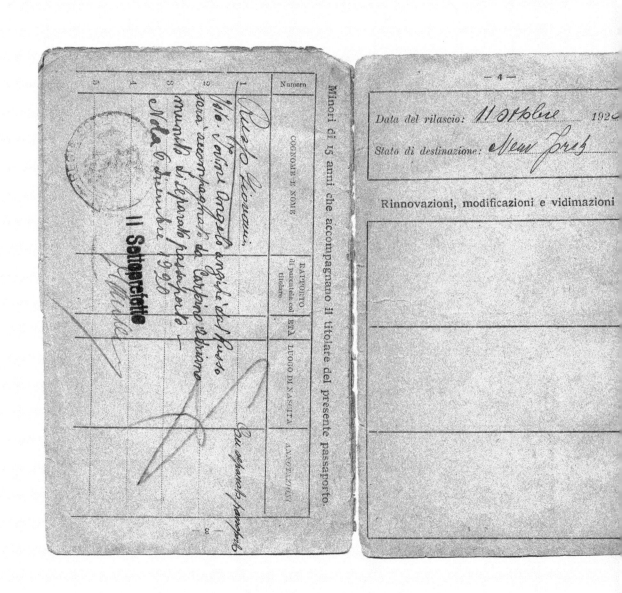

Data del rilascio: *11 ottobre* 192___

Stato di destinazione: *New York*

Rinnovazioni, modificazioni e vidimazioni

Minori di 15 anni che accompagnano il titolare del presente passaporto.

Numero	COGNOME E NOME	RAPPORTO di parentela col titolare	ETÀ	LUOGO DI NASCITA	ANNOTAZIONI
1	*Russo Giovanni*				
2					
3					
4					
5					

Il Sottoprefetto

Acknowledgements

Francesco would like to thank the following people:
My Grandparents & Parents for creating all the amazing memories which is the foundation for this book.
My sisters Maria and Christine for all the pictures and endless supply of support.
Gina for listening and her honesty.
Amanda for the helping me with the title.

Ashley would like to thank the following people:
My husband Bojan for always having my back and believing in me.
Damion Tedeschi for making our gorgeous cover, website, and everything else along the way.
Christopher "Fran" Sciacco who told Francesco he knew the perfect writer for him.
My family, who supports me through everything.